# I'm Juggling As Fast As I Can!

## Managing Stress, Avoiding Burnout and Achieving Balance

 Denny Kercher

Chrysalis Publishing
418 Blue Lake Trail
Lafayette, CO 80026
303-926-7279
dkercher@aol.com

Design by Concepts Unlimited.

Published by:
Chrysalis Publishing
418 Blue Lake Trail
Lafayette, CO 80026
303-926-7279
dkercher@aol.com

ISBN 0-9755709-0-0

# DEDICATION

To Heidi and Renny

with overwhelming love and gratitude.

# A Word of Thanks

This book has been built on the shoulders of many who have been trailblazers before me—the many people who have written their books in the hope of giving insight into better ways of managing one's life. All of their stories and wisdom have helped me grow emotionally and spiritually and have formed the backbone of my experiences that I share with you. I acknowledge and thank all of them for their contribution.

A huge thank you to all of my friends who have loved and encouraged me over the years. What would the world be without friends? My long-time friend, Barbara Lamm, who read my very first manuscript years ago and without devastating me, let me know that it was not "quite right." Barbara has been with me through many milestones in my life and will always be my forever friend. My dear friend, Kris Whorton, who has been unfailing in her encouragement and love—always letting me know that she believed in me and that the book was worth writing. There are no words to describe my gratitude to my friends, Russ and Carol Olin, who have taught me so much about how to live a rich, just and ethical life and are my dearest friends who have been a constant source of support and encouragement to me.

Thank you to Nicky Marone who began the editing process of the book until her own book demanded more of her attention. She gave me wonderful direction for the first three chapters of the book. And, to Pam McKinnie of Concepts Unlimited, who has been with me through the final birthing process. Pam has become not only a professional colleague with great skill, but a dear friend as well.

I could never have seen the birth of this book without the support of Josie and Rollie Heath. They believed in me and the potential of the book and helped me to see it finally come to be.

Last but not least, I thank my beautiful and wonderful family—Lisa Sveland, my niece and my "third daughter," her husband Chris, my sister Cheryl, who has shared so many of my experiences growing up and my Down's Syndrome brother, Scotty, who taught me the meaning of unmitigated delight. I am especially grateful for my son-in-law, Lance Kercher-Pratt, who is the wonderful and loving son I never had, and the priceless gift to all of us, my granddaughter Brooke, who keeps me focused on what is really meaningful in life!

This book is dedicated to my two daughters, Renny and Heidi, who everyone who knows me knows, are my very best friends. I will forever be grateful to their father for giving me these two precious human beings who grew up with me and unconditionally love me.

# TABLE OF CONTENTS

# UNDERSTANDING THE DILEMMA

*Wholeness or well-being is not the absence of brokenness.*
*Instead it is what you choose, at the center of your life,*
*to do with your brokenness.*
Howard Clinebell

Once I read a book by Sark (yes, just one name) called *The Inspiration Sandwich.* She stated that writing a book is like writing a love letter. That resonated with me because that is how I feel about this book. I have been in the process of writing this book for many years. Originally, it was full of dry "to-do's." I then decided that I wanted it to be more conversational, more like a letter. So this is my love letter to you.

My daughters are grown, and I'm left with my dog. I don't have the stress and strain of day care, school, after school activities, work schedules and the demands of fixing dinner, etc.; but I did. Through my work I have talked to hundreds of families who have shared their stories with me and with their information and mine, I have learned some helpful things that I trust will help you.

The work I do involves organizational consulting, training and speaking. In the over 25 years of being in this business, I have worked in hundreds of different organizations, from high-tech and scientific, to heavy construction and manufacturing. The list encompasses small companies, large organizations, government agencies, non-profits and corporations. I think I have just about seen it all. I've seen good managers and bad ones, excellent companies and failing ones. I've seen wonderful and productive employees flourish under self-serving, arrogant managers. I've seen wonderful companies go down in spite of their great values, benefits and employees. I've seen optimistic and positive people come from the most dysfunctional environments…and I've seen very unfortunate dysfunctional people come from very loving and healthy environments. I'm not a scientist so I can't talk about genetics or why certain individuals are more "resilient" than others. I can talk "turkey" about what works on a day to day basis to get us through whatever circumstance is in front of us.

We are unsure about everything: relationships, jobs, health, world stability, you name it. And of course we are overwhelmed, over-stimulated, over-worked and over-tired. Welcome to the 21st Century.

I hear people complain of being tired, scared and depressed. Everyone is juggling as fast as they can, and at the same time trying to maintain a sense of composure, equilibrium and poise. Many times I have looked up at Whatever pleading in distress for a mommy to comfort and support me and a dad to fix everything because I feel so overwhelmed. Well, no such luck. So how do we manage this crazy time we're in?

When people write books, it's usually because a theme is burning inside. That yearning which needs to be expressed comes from a profound experience, or a series of profound experiences, that cause one to need to write it down, either to challenge, entertain, enlighten, or just to exorcise a nagging demon. The insights I share have aided me in managing my own challenging life situations and are a result of years of informal research, study and application. I can't tell you how many books and articles I have read over the years written by experts to help me understand what my problem is and how to live with it. I'm supposed to be positive, optimistic, not worry, manage my stress and live a balanced life. I'm not supposed to worry about tomorrow because "tomorrow will take care of itself." I'm supposed to look at the bright side and if I ever think negative thoughts then whamo, those negative thoughts will become a self-fulfilling prophecy. No matter what I do, I'm doing it wrong.

Well, I do worry, I do get stressed, I do struggle with depression, I do have negative tapes that run through my head, I don't always eat right and I don't exercise every day. I wonder every month if I'll have business next month. I have lived the gamut between living my life successfully and not so successfully. I have done and said things for which I am truly ashamed, and have had other fleeting moments of angelic behavior that I wished everyone would notice. "So," you ask, "why should I read your book?" Precisely because I am just like you! I get overwhelmed, depressed, scared and experience every other negative feeling that plagues us as humans. **However,** when I'm in the midst of depression or worry or beating myself up, I've learned some skills that help me get through it. Some of these techniques I've learned myself and others I have learned from many people I have met throughout my life. I also have learned from those experts I have read. Over the past 25 years, I have shared these techniques with thousands of people who find themselves stressed and burned out and their lives hopelessly out of balance. Although there are so many books out there about stress, burnout and balance, this book is written with simplicity and clarity and I hope you will find something helpful and affirming for you.

If you are reading this book, you probably are one of us who is trying to juggle all areas of your life so that you can "have it all and do it all." We want to have exciting careers where we are acknowledged for our unique contribution to our job, a personal life full of adventure and meaning, quality time with children who are brilliant and charming, an active and stimulating social life, an intimate relationship that is satisfying and close to perfect. Instead we are anxious about being laid off and so exhausted at the end of the day that exercise, cooking a gourmet meal and meditation are out of the question. More often than not we throw something on the table from the grocery store deli for dinner. Intimate time alone and making love with a spouse or significant other has become a fantasy, and quality time with children is found in the car driving to and from little league, ballet and music lessons. Balancing one's external life is a worthy notion, but in my experience, it cannot happen until the internal life is more balanced. So the first place to focus is on the inside. I am not implying that this book will make you internally balanced in order to be balanced externally. My goal is to bring attention to the various segments of our lives that make up the whole of who we are, because ignoring any one of these parts will over time create stress.

Managing stress, avoiding burnout and achieving wholeness involves attention to the seven most important areas of our lives: 1) physical health and well being, 2) emotional understanding and control, 3) spiritual health, 4) intellectual pursuit and

challenge, 5) family and social relationships, 6) career
satisfaction and 7) soul discovery.

In order to balance these areas of our lives, we need to know
what gets us off track in the first place. What goes on in our
deeper selves? What makes us tick? Why do we feel happy and
exhilarated one minute and hostile and aggressive the next? We
are not mentally deranged or un-whole because we experience
negative emotions. We are not unbalanced if we have a bad day.
We are just human! We don't have to hide who we are and what
we experience by faking a "happy face." In today's world of a
quick fix, people anxiously look for a solution to the confusion
and pain caused by stress, trying dieting, drugs, psychotherapy,
changing jobs, houses, or spouses. Nothing seems to result in
more than a temporary fix. Understanding our interior dynamics
is the first step to bringing harmony, wholeness and balance to
the seven areas of our lives.

In Chapters 1 - 3, we will begin to understand the causes of
stress and burnout. These chapters provide simple analogies to
explain the origins of stress and how to take preventative meas-
ures to stop the downward cycle. These chapters also explain
how prolonged stress leads to the devastating illness of burnout,
which is pervasive and can debilitate people for the rest of their
lives. We will learn how to recognize the symptoms at each stage
of burnout and understand the harmful effects on our body.

Chapters 4 - 9 help us to begin the healing process by understanding each of the seven areas—our physical, emotional, spirit,
intellectual, relationships, career and soul—in order to experience
how the pieces fit together to create our whole Self. Understanding and addressing each aspect, a piece at a time, makes the
task of self-healing less overwhelming.

At the end of each chapter, I have included a list of references.
I am familiar with these references and have included them
because I have found them helpful as it relates to the content of
the specific chapter.

Many who pick up this book will read it for help in the
process of discovery. Others will read it to give insight into how
they might help a fellow worker, a spouse, significant other,

friend, parent, or child. My fervent desire is that you will find the book truly helpful in your own search for balance and joy.

Let me assure you, again, that this book is not about finding a way to get rid of stress forever. It's about finding ways to deal with it on a day-to-day basis. It also is about finding proactive ways to make our lives less stressful. Understanding and accommodating our emotional, physical and spirit needs helps us to lessen the stress that we encounter every day.

Publishing this book is a project that I want to open up to my readers. As you are reading the book and you think of things that you would like expanded upon, coping methods you have learned, or whatever you would like to see included in a book of this nature, please write me at dkercher@aol.com. I will include your ideas, comments and lessons in the next edition.

# PART I

# TELLING YOUR STORY

*Is there ever any particular spot*
*where one can put one's finger and say,*
*"It all began that day, at such a time*
*and such a place, with such an incident"?*
Agatha Christie

*Cherria,*
*"Father Give*
*me Back my*
*other leg"*

*To have one's individuality completely ignored*
*is like being pushed quite out of life.*
*Like being blown out as one blows out a light*
Evelyn Scott

When I was growing up I loved to listen to my aunt and mother talk at the kitchen table about their childhood memories. My mother was the oldest of four children and was afflicted with nerve deafness when she turned 15 years old. It was very traumatic for her to leave her family in South Dakota to go to deaf school in Gooding, Idaho. Many of the deaf from that school moved to Spokane, Washington, during the depression because there were jobs for the deaf in lumber mills and at the printing presses of the local newspapers. She met my father there and they were married in 1938. My father was also deaf and quite a bit older than my mother. Since my mother was such a "catch" she married the one man who had a job at that time, although she always believed he was beneath her. She was never happy and struggled with bitterness, anger and depression all of her life.

The only time there was laughter in the house was when my aunt (her sister) would come to visit. Those wonderful times, watching my aunt finger sign the words to my mother, my mother talking back in her high-pitched, kind of squeaky voice, both of them laughing hysterically about growing up on the farm, taught me how important it is to tell stories that recall fond, warm and funny memories. I know that those times of hilarity at the kitchen table were what kept my aunt and mother able to cope with their very difficult and painful circumstances at the time.

Every once in a while they would include me in their memories and explain certain events so that I, too, could laugh hysterically along with them. It felt good to be included and it felt good to hear the stories about how life was when my mother was growing up. Sometimes they would talk about very ugly memories and tell sad and bitter stories, but somehow when they said good-bye to each other at the end of the day, they both walked away feeling much better. I remember mom being kinder, warmer and gentler after these visits. She seemed calmed and renewed in her spirit able to face another day.

There is something very healing about telling our stories because it helps us to understand how and why we developed our own perceptions, beliefs and values about ourselves and others. The reality of our experiences often is skewed through the lenses of our perceptions about them. The interpretations we make about the perception of events throughout our lives often become more understandable when we begin to consciously remember and talk about them.

For example, if you and I are on a roller coaster together and I am terrified and you are having the time of your life, is it the

roller coaster that is stressful? If you and I are being laid off from the same company and I can take it in stride, whereas you become overwhelmed with anxiety attacks, is it the layoff that is stressful? If someone we know seems to travel along life's path, taking things in stride, whereas we beat ourselves up and are filled with worry, is it life that is stressful? In these examples, we can see that it is not the roller coaster, the company, or life that is stressful. It is our perception of those events that causes us stress. The perception of life events lies in the eyes of the beholder. To begin to manage the stress in our life, we have to first change the way we think about it. In order to do that, it is helpful to know how we built those thoughts and perceptions in the first place. That's why it is important to tell our story.

# Exercise-Telling Your Story

My daughter, Heidi, is fanatical about pictures. When you walk into her house you see pictures everywhere of everyone who is important in her life. She has pictures of me and her dad, grandparents, friends, her daughter and husband and many family members. I have found a wonderful kind of comfort in looking at all of those pictures—people who are smiling out of the frames with their special significance to my daughter. Each of those pictures tells a story. Each of the people in those pictures has contributed to Heidi's story. Those smiling people have impacted my daughter and molded her into the person she is today. They give her a touchstone, a reminder of roots and stability and of the people who love her.

How about you? Find as many baby and childhood pictures as possible. Find a tablet and pencil and begin to write. Who is that little person in your childhood pictures— that little boy with the baseball cap, smudged knee and bandaged eye, or that little girl in the new pinafore holding the cat by the head? How did you think of yourself physically? What did you look like? How tall were you? What did you do in school? What subjects did you like? What did you do with your feelings? Capturing the memories of who you were as a child and teenager helps you to understand how significant events impact your perception of yourself as an adult.

As you consider each decade of your life (1 - 12, teens, 20's, 30's, etc.), recall the events, the pain and joy that contributed to your life. Examine the lessons you learned, and how the many aspects of your Self developed. Tell about parents, friends, grandparents, sisters and brothers. What did they teach you—good and not so good? Who were you as you were growing up? Write as many things as you can possibly remember that contributed to who you are now. It will help to provide some objectivity as to why you have the perceptions you do and why you think the way you do. This kind of self-reflection begins to open the door of understanding to the sources of the stress in your life.

When I look back at my own story and see my own pictures, when I share those stories with my family, I realize how my past perceptions have left an indelible mark on me in how I view things today. So when things happen to me they are filtered through the unique glasses of my perception which may or may not be objective. Telling my story helps me gain a better objective perspective and gives me greater understanding about why I am the way I am. When I know that, or see that, I can begin to make concrete behavioral changes.

I grew up believing my mother never loved me. I have gone over and over my memories and I can never remember a time when she said, "I love you." I do remember every beating, every cruel word and her rejection of me. I know, intellectually, that she loved me as best she could under her difficult circumstances, but through my perceptions, I believed that if my own mother couldn't love me, then I was pretty bad. Compounding those perceptions, starting as a little girl, it seemed that I was prey to many men who abused me sexually and verbally. The rejection from my mother created an insatiable need to be loved and affirmed and made me always fearful of rejection. The sexual abuse from men made me believe that if anything was wrong in the relationship, it was obviously my fault.

These experiences have created "stress triggers" which are clearly related to whether I perceive people like me or not. If I perceive that people don't like me, or that I have not pleased them, I immediately believe it is my fault. So my life has been a constant dance of trying to please people. Since I never believed I could possibly please anyone, I lived in agony that it was not only my fault, but that I was bad, therefore I was hopeless.

Telling and writing my story have given me an opportunity to see how those experiences left me with perceptions about myself and my relationship with others that are not really true. I know now that when I become the most anxious and stressed it's because I perceive I'm being rejected or that I'm not loved. This emotional reaction could be called one of my "stress trigger points." I become and stay anxious until I perceive that the relationship is okay.

To help us find our "stress triggers" by telling our stories, I would like to explore with you what I call our Seven Areas of Wholeness. Exploring each of the seven areas separately through the following questionnaire helps us to understand how they contribute to our uniqueness and wholeness and to also see in what areas our particular "stress triggers" might lie. Each of the chapters will then explore each area of wholeness in order to find specific ways to reduce stress and create balance.

## SEVEN AREAS OF WHOLENESS

The following questions are given as a guide to help you find your own specific and unique answers to your stories and also to identify the areas where your stress triggers are the most troubling. Take as much or as little time as you like. When you begin to read the chapter that corresponds with one of the areas of wholeness, it might be helpful to review what the most stressful triggers are for you.

## SEVEN AREAS OF WHOLENESS
### QUESTIONNAIRE

### Physical Concept and Well-Being

We all wish we had a body that met some standard that we, or others, have set for us. Using the following questions, tell your story of how your perceptions of yourself have directly impacted how healthy your body is today.

On a scale of 1 to 4, rate the degree of stress each of the following statements causes in you today.

| | Not Stressful.......Very Stressful | | | |
|---|---|---|---|---|
| | 1 | 2 | 3 | 4 |
| 1. I am easily stressed because of my body | | | | |
| 2. I believe I am too fat or too thin | | | | |
| 3. My eating habits stress me | | | | |
| 4. I do not groom myself as well as I could | | | | |
| 5. I do not exercise properly | | | | |
| 6. I indulge in harmful addictions | | | | |
| 7. I sleep well | | | | |
| 8. I am comfortable in my own skin | | | | |
| 9. I pay attention to my physical needs | | | | |

Remember those areas that are particularly stressful to you. When you read the chapter on physical concept and well-being, look for ways to reduce stress in this area.

## Emotional Control and Well-Being

Managing our emotions can be a major source of stress. As you answer these questions, think about the events and memories in your life that have contributed to your emotional growth and maturity and cause you to react the way you do to life around you now.

On a scale of 1 to 4, rate the degree of stress each of the following statements causes in you today.

| | Not Stressful.......Very Stressful | | | |
|---|---|---|---|---|
| | 1 | 2 | 3 | 4 |
| 1. I am comfortable with how I manage my feelings | | | | |
| 2. I am emotional | | | | |
| 3. I manage negative feelings | | | | |
| 5. I get physically angry, verbally explosive, cry or violent when angry | | | | |
| 6. When I'm angry I am stressed | | | | |
| 7. I manage my emotions appropriately | | | | |
| 8. I talk to those with whom I'm angry | | | | |
| 9. I am uncomfortable when I'm angry | | | | |
| 10. I am afraid of being hurt in relationships | | | | |
| 11. I share intimate feelings easily | | | | |
| 12. I am uncomfortable with other people's emotions | | | | |

Remember those areas that are particularly stressful to you. When you read the chapter on emotional control and well-being, look for ways to reduce stress in this area.

### Understanding Spirit Needs

The next area of wholeness is the Spirit, which may be difficult to grasp. It's the part of us that houses our personality, our values, beliefs and attitudes. It is the foundation of our Self that motivates our thinking and behavior. Using the following questions, tell your story by thinking about the events and memories in your life that have contributed to the strengths or needs of your spirit.

| | Not Stressful.......Very Stressful | | | |
| --- | --- | --- | --- | --- |
| | 1 | 2 | 3 | 4 |
| 1. I am worthwhile | | | | |
| 2. I am valued | | | | |
| 3. My life is meaningful | | | | |
| 4. I make a meaningful contribution in my circle of influence | | | | |
| 5. In my world I am secure: | | | | |
| • Physically | | | | |
| • Emotionally | | | | |
| • Financially | | | | |
| • Sexually | | | | |
| • Mentally | | | | |
| 6. I believe I am competent in my job | | | | |
| 7. I believe I am competent as a mother or father | | | | |
| 8. I believe I am competent as a child to my own parents | | | | |
| 9. I believe I am competent in my personal endeavors | | | | |
| 10. I have a trusting relationship with my spouse or significant other | | | | |
| 11. I have trusting relationships with friends | | | | |
| 12. It is easy for me to trust others | | | | |
| 13. I have a significant loving relationship | | | | |
| 14. I enjoy giving and receiving love | | | | |
| 15. I know that I am loved by the important people in my life | | | | |

Remember those areas that are particularly stressful to you. When you read the chapter on understanding spirit needs, look for ways to reduce stress in this area.

## Intellectual Stimulation and Expansion

It is important that the mind never stops exploring new thoughts and ideas. It's that creativity that helps to keep our minds vital, adding productivity and longevity to our lives. However, if we have been taught negative beliefs, we might not be able to rid our mind of obsessive thoughts which get in the way of our ability to be creative and productive. Using the following questions, tell your story by thinking about the events and memories in your life that have contributed to the way you value and use your mind.

On a scale of 1 to 4, rate the degree of stress each of the following statements causes in you today.

| | Not Stressful.......Very Stressful | | | |
| --- | --- | --- | --- | --- |
| | 1 | 2 | 3 | 4 |
| 1. I have obsessive thoughts | | | | |
| 2. I believe my mind is healthy | | | | |
| 3. I am able to focus on projects | | | | |
| 4. I like to search for new ideas | | | | |
| 5. I like to solve problems | | | | |
| 6. I allow myself to be creative | | | | |
| 7. I am not troubled by recurring thoughts | | | | |
| 8. I enjoy learning | | | | |

Remember those areas that are particularly stressful to you. When you read the chapter on intellectual stimulation and expansion, look for ways to reduce stress in this area.

## Family and Social Relationships

Relationships can be the source of major stress triggers. Our life experiences and messages we received have impacted how we relate to others in our lives now. Using the following questions tell your story by thinking about the events and memories in your life that have contributed to the quality and satisfaction of your relationships.

On a scale of 1 to 4, rate the degree of stress each of the following statements causes in you today.

| | Not Stressful.......Very Stressful | | | |
| --- | :-: | :-: | :-: | :-: |
| | 1 | 2 | 3 | 4 |
| 1. I am comfortable in my relationship with my spouse or significant other | | | | |
| 2. I am comfortable in my relationship with my children | | | | |
| 3. I am comfortable in my relationship with my parents | | | | |
| 4. I am comfortable in my relationships with my close friends | | | | |
| 5. I make friends easily | | | | |
| 6. I like to entertain | | | | |
| 7. My spouse or significant other likes me | | | | |
| 8. My children like me | | | | |
| 9. My friends like me | | | | |

Remember those areas that are particularly stressful to you. When you read the chapter on family and social relationships, look for ways to reduce stress in this area.

### Job, Career, Professional Contribution

Our jobs and careers contribute greatly to our sense of meaning and can be our greatest source of stress. Using the following questions tell your story by thinking about the events and memories in your life that have contributed to the quality and satisfaction of your job, career or profession.

On a scale of 1 to 4, rate the degree of stress each of the following statements causes in you today.

|  | Not Stressful.......Very Stressful | | | |
|  | 1 | 2 | 3 | 4 |
|---|---|---|---|---|
| 1. My job is meaningful to me | | | | |
| 2. My supervisor respects me | | | | |
| 3. My co-workers respect me | | | | |
| 4. I get along with my co-workers | | | | |
| 5. I am proud of the work I do | | | | |
| 6. I like working in my company | | | | |
| 7. I like working with others | | | | |
| 8. We have fun and laugh at work | | | | |
| 9. I know what my boss expects from me | | | | |
| 10. I know what my co-workers expect from me | | | | |
| 11. Others know my expectations | | | | |
| 12. I have other job options if I want to quit my job | | | | |

Remember those areas that are particularly stressful to you. When you read the chapter on job, career, professional contribution, look for ways to reduce stress in this area.

### Soul Discovery

Considering our soul defines our perception of meaningfulness. In turning our focus inward to the inexplicable principles that guide us, it helps to reflect on what that power is and how it contributes to our peace and serenity in the midst of stress. Using the following questions, tell your story by thinking about the events and memories in your life that have contributed to your degree of comfort in your understanding of your soul.

Remember those areas that are particularly stressful to you. When you read the chapter on Soul Discovery, look for ways to reduce stress in this area.

On a scale of 1 to 4, rate the degree of stress each of the following statements causes in you today.

|  | Not Stressful.......Very Stressful | | | |
| --- | --- | --- | --- | --- |
|  | 1 | 2 | 3 | 4 |
| 1.  I have a sense of awe/wonder about life |  |  |  |  |
| 2.  My life is meaningful to me |  |  |  |  |
| 3.  I am comfortable with the mysteriousness of life |  |  |  |  |
| 4.  I question why bad things happen |  |  |  |  |
| 5.  I know I am guided by a Power greater than myself |  |  |  |  |
| 6.  I am maximizing my potential |  |  |  |  |
| 7.  I am comfortable that I am making a meaningful contribution to life |  |  |  |  |
| 8.  I believe that God is loving not punishing |  |  |  |  |
| 9.  I believe that God is the divine source within me |  |  |  |  |
| 10.  I am not afraid of death |  |  |  |  |

Remember those areas that are particularly stressful to you. When you read the chapter on Soul Discovery, look for ways to reduce stress in this area.

When you have thoughtfully gone through this exercise, you'll find your stress triggers, and you will have a better sense of what is present and what is missing in the seven areas of wholeness. This exercise in self-reflection will illuminate the areas that are painful and most stress producing in your life. When we keep these insights in mind, we are more sensitive to ideas on how to manage those particular parts of our lives. Keep your notes accessible as we journey through this book. This knowledge will help as we explore the ways that healing can begin within these seven areas.

*References:* To learn the importance of telling stories, read the series of books about *Chicken Soup for the Soul* or *Kitchen Table Wisdom.* We find comfort in listening to stories. What are the stories that touch you? What kind of stories make the most impact on you?

# UNDERSTANDING SELF
## Origin and Dynamics of Stress

*I can stand what I know.*
*It's what I don't know that frightens me.*
Francis Newton

*Sometimes when I consider what tremendous consequences*
*come from little things...I am tempted to think...*
*there are no little things.*
Bruce Barton

## ORIGIN OF STRESS

In order to understand stress, we need to start at the beginning. As we can see by the diagram, the stress cycle begins when we don't know what's going on—***being overwhelmed,*** and ***being uncertain.***

Not knowing what is going to happen, being ***overwhelmed*** and ***uncertain*** with responsibilities at work and home,

which leads to a feeling of being ***out of control***,

which leads to a feeling of being ***vulnerable or afraid,***

which leads to STRESS!

It seems that everyone I meet has no idea what tomorrow will bring and certainly is overwhelmed. In fact when I ask people how they are, the first thing out of their mouths is, "busy." I don't think I have met anyone who has said they have nothing to do. Sometimes I wonder if we are not all in contests with each other to see who is the busiest…it's almost a badge of honor. We measure our self worth by how busy we are. If someone else is busier than we are then it might mean they are more productive, or more worthwhile. However, it's this "busy-ness" that is contributing to our being overwhelmed.

Uncertainty, or not knowing what is going to happen next or not being able to understand what is happening around us, is the other contributor to becoming stressed. Certainly we can list all of the things that we don't know—what will happen tomorrow, what will happen with our jobs, our children, our friends, our health. The list is endless. Any kind of change in our lives also creates uncertainty because it means we don't know what we can count on and it throws us out of our comfort zone. It is like letting go of one trapeze to fly through the air of uncertainty, just to grab on to the new trapeze which is also uncertain.

Even if a change in our lives is a positive one, we can be overwhelmed with anxiety because we don't know how to predict the impact of that change on our lives. Getting married, having a baby, buying a new house, car, or moving to a new location is exciting and challenging, but it can also be stressful because we don't know if we can manage the change. Difficult changes—divorce, death, loss of a job, or a relationship, health or youth, also cause stress because, again, we don't know what the next step will be. Since most of us are in constant major life fluctuations, it is no wonder we are experiencing major stress most of the time.

Not only are we overwhelmed and uncertain by things happening to us personally, we are also overwhelmed by the massive changes in the world, our organizations, in technology and our jobs. We have more to do and less time to do it. Even though we have to do it faster, we are still expected to do it perfectly. Rarely do we know if the priority job we are working on today will be the priority job tomorrow. Just when we believe we have the skills and resources we need to accomplish the tasks in front of us, we realize the rules have changed and that perhaps we don't have a grasp of what is happening at all.

This feeling of being overwhelmed and uncertain lead to the next step in the stress cycle, which is feeling out of control. This lack of control is experienced in degrees, from a vague feeling of discomfort to major distress, anxiety and panic. Most of us have learned to live with this, but mental and emotional breakdowns result when we believe we no longer have control over *any* aspect of our lives. The diseases of the new century—anorexia, bulimia, and obsessive compulsive disorders—are related to peoples' need to control some small portion of their lives when all else seems totally out of control.

Think about every time you've been stressed. It almost always is about the control we believe we have or do not have, over the events that are happening around us. So, if that is where stress really begins, we need to learn what thinking and behavior we need to control in ourselves to lessen stress and how to control it. If we don't believe we have any control over ourselves, the result is often a constant nagging sense of anxiety and vulnerability. This fearfulness may not be apparent to others, but it is very apparent to those of us who are experiencing it. Vulnerability is always there, scratching in the recesses of the mind, becoming that shadowy annoying companion because we always know that a time is coming when we will, again, be out of control.

So, here is the crux of the matter. When we find ourselves constantly struggling with not knowing from one day to the next what's going to happen, when we feel we have little control over our lives, when we struggle with trying to be positive, when we are feeling afraid and vulnerable, when this occurs over a prolonged period of time, then the result is a complete depletion of internal (or psychic) energy. It's this process that becomes a downward spiral leading to stress. We cannot continually go through this stress cycle without paying a price. The price we pay is in being zapped of our internal energy.

## DYNAMICS OF HUMAN NATURE
### Iceberg Analogy: Conscious & Subconscious

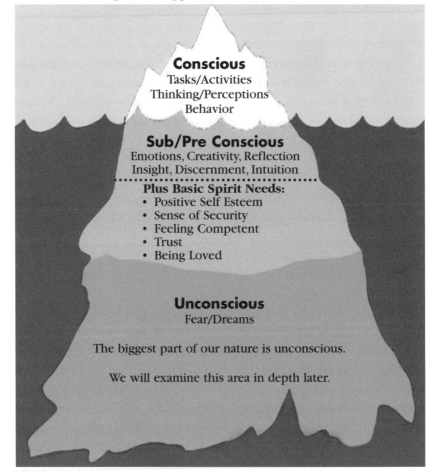

**Conscious**
Tasks/Activities
Thinking/Perceptions
Behavior

**Sub/Pre Conscious**
Emotions, Creativity, Reflection
Insight, Discernment, Intuition
**Plus Basic Spirit Needs:**
• Positive Self Esteem
• Sense of Security
• Feeling Competent
• Trust
• Being Loved

**Unconscious**
Fear/Dreams

The biggest part of our nature is unconscious.

We will examine this area in depth later.

Now that we have seen how feeling overwhelmed and uncertain leads to stress, it is necessary to see how it impacts us internally. To explain the internal dynamics of human beings and to convey the role of the seven attributes of wholeness, an iceberg analogy, (shown on the preceding page) is particularly appropriate. Icebergs often grow to be very large, but most of their mass lies beneath the surface of the water, hidden from view. The same holds true for human beings. Our visible self, that is, our conscious words and behaviors are minuscule compared to what lies in our sub-conscious and unconscious. As the figure illustrates, the tip of the iceberg is but one small portion of the self and is where conscious activity takes place. This conscious activity involves the tasks that we do on a day-to-day basis and includes our intellectual, thinking and reasoning activity. It also manifests in what we say and how we behave. Yet, it is only a very small segment of our total being. While at work or in our personal relationships, we only see the tip of the other person's iceberg. And they only see the tip of our iceberg. Or, in other words, we see each other's behaviors and hear the words. We really don't know what is going on underneath at the deeper levels.

Most of us put a lot of energy into the tasks and activities that must be done at the moment. We do not pay a lot of attention to the stuff that is going on in our subconscious. And, we're certainly not inclined to pay a whole lot of attention to what might be going on in someone else's subconscious. We usually only react to what we see on the conscious level—people's behavior and words—which may or may not give clues as to what might be going on under the surface.

In fact, I knew a man who was part of a crew that inspected gas pipelines. This crew of seven had been together for over 27 years, went hunting and fishing together and were very good friends. They lived in a small community so their wives were also good friends and their kids grew up together. One night this man went into his garage, took a gun and shot himself to death. Everyone who knew him was stunned and shocked. No one had a clue what was really going on inside him. Many of us may believe that we know the people we are close to and that we understand them. We believe we know our spouses, our children, our friends and parents. It is really not true, of course. In fact, we may not even know ourselves.

So let's put on our scuba gear and dive below the surface of the conscious into the sub-conscious area as shown in the iceberg figure. As you can see, the subconscious is home to a lot of activity including our emotions, feelings, intuition and creative abilities as well as our spirit needs.

Many of us work hard to make sure our emotions don't slip up and come to the surface inadvertently displaying themselves in negative behavior. We take classes and read books to learn to control our emotions so we are seen as mature and professional. But it is important to pay attention to our emotions, feelings and intuition because they are the windows to our spirit. Emotions are the nerve endings that send out warning signals to our conscious level to tell us that we are experiencing either pain or joy in our spirit. When one or more of our spirit needs is missing, the spirit is in pain. Then our emotions act like nerve endings to reveal that pain at the conscious level, just like our nerve endings in our body tell us when our body is in pain. That is why when our emotions may be fluctuating wildly in the subconscious, it often shows up in unpredictable behavior at the conscious level.

One hour our self-esteem (one of our spirit needs) may be soaring because of some nice thing someone has said to us—our emotions are happy and joyful manifesting in positive words or behavior. The next hour, we may be in the doldrums because someone did not acknowledge us as we expected resulting in negative words or behavior. Our emotions are the messengers that tell us when a need in our spirit has been compromised or when it has been fulfilled. Therefore, when you see negative behavior or words at the tip of the iceberg, you can be assured that the source is underneath the surface.

Often we are surprised when we find ourselves behaving in a negative way. Because our spirit needs are in the sub-conscious, we may not be consciously aware when those needs are or are not being met. We don't get the "clue" until we notice something in our behavior and have no idea where it came from or why we reacted so negatively.

If we say critical things about our spouse or significant other, for example, even though we might believe the criticism is legitimate, the real reason we are critical is often a nagging fear that our spouse doesn't love us as much as we think he or she should. Or worse, we might be afraid that our spouse is secretly criticizing us! Sometimes we behave poorly toward our children by heaping words of criticism or physical abuse on them. On the surface, or in our conscious level, we say it's because we are trying to civilize them, but it might actually be because we are afraid that we will be seen as incompetent parents if we cannot control our children.

In order to clearly understand the meaning of our negative behavior, it is important that we understand the needs of our spirit and how when those needs are not met emotional reactions are triggered. Whenever we behave negatively, whether through our words or actions, it is because one or more of our spirit needs has not been met.

To further understand how subconscious activity impacts the conscious and unconscious, let's use an example of being asked by your boss to complete a project by Friday night. You work very hard to do an outstanding job and are relieved when it is laid on her desk. On Monday morning when you come to work, you see an email that says, "Please see me A.S.A.P. regarding report." What do you think? Usually, the first thing we think about is "Uh oh, I'm in trouble now!" Why do we always go right to the negative? Why wouldn't we believe we were going to be praised for the great job we did? Because most of us have a little creature that sits on our shoulder with her mouth glued to our ear who chatters all day telling us about all of the things we should have and shouldn't have done. She loves to tell us when we are in "real trouble." Her name is Polly Paranoid. Polly Paranoid continually attacks our five spirit needs—self esteem, security, competency, trust and love. Peering under the surface with your scuba gear and goggles, we see her telling us that we didn't do the report right, we're stupid, we're incompetent and so on.

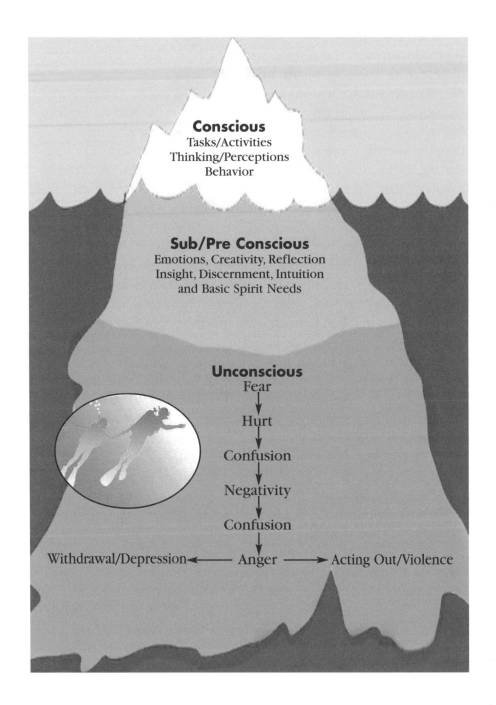

All of us struggle to one degree or another with the fear of uncertainty. We have no guarantees about life. We don't know if we, or any of our loved ones, will be with us tomorrow or if we are carrying around a terminal disease. If we brood about it, we can truly become nonfunctional. That does not mean, however, that the fear is not there lurking in our unconscious causing a kind of chain reaction. When that fear begins to attack one of the needs of the spirit, it comes up into the layer of the emotions or feelings, and then, horror of horrors, often explodes through the surface into our consciousness where it displays itself in our behavior. Many times these behaviors are inappropriate and nega-tive causing us embarrassment, confusion and pain.

This is the story of my life. Polly Paranoid has a front row seat on my shoulder. I'm always jumping hoops in my mind believing that everything Polly Paranoid tells me is the truth about me. Emotionally, I am experiencing intense anxiety and stress. Now, does anyone in my world know that's going on with me? No, because I know how to pretend that I'm okay on the surface or at the conscious level. I know how to behave. I know how to func-tion without laying out all of those negative feelings for everyone to see.

Now what do I do with those negative feelings? I stuff them in a "nit" bag. I think we all have "nit" bags. We can't see them, but we know they're there. Sometimes instead of clarifying with people what I perceive in light of the other's behaviors, I just stuff it. Well, guess what? If we continue down that unconscious fear cycle, the hurt becomes confusion, the confusion becomes nega-tivity and the negativity becomes anger.

And anger can show up in variances of two extremes—one extreme is acting out or violent behavior, and the other extreme is withdrawal or depression. When we are angry, the emotions bub-ble up through the surface showing up in behavior anywhere along a continuum from someone who is "in your face," or, con-versely, is more and more introverted and withdrawn. *Remember, this stress reaction starts under the surface when we believe that one or more of our spirit needs are not being met.*

So, looking at what's going on underneath the iceberg we discover that when we unconsciously fear that our spirit needs are compromised, it leads to negative emotions (in the sub-conscious) that lead to negative behavior (in the conscious). We expend so much energy trying to manage all of this that we finally reach a point when we become physically, emotionally and mentally exhausted. Our Self quits. We experience a total loss of energy. This is called burnout.

*References:* Seaward, Brian Luke. *Managing Stress: Principles and Strategies for Health and Well Being.* Luke is a friend of mine and has written a most wonderful complete book on the impact of stress on health and whole-ness. It is used as a textbook at the University of Colorado.

Clinebell, Howard. *Well Being:* I find myself going back and reading this book often. There are a lot of little tests and simple stories that are uplifting.

# 3 UNDERSTANDING BURNOUT

*Character cannot be developed in ease and quiet. Only through experience of trial and suffering can the soul be strengthened, vision cleared, ambition inspired and success achieved.*
Helen Keller

Not long ago a friend, who is vice president of an organization, called to tell me about a little test that appeared in the Sunday paper to determine whether one was burned out. He said that for kicks he took the test and found that he marked every single question indicating that he was severely burned out. He said that even the things that he used to love to do were not fun anymore. That lament has been shared with me countless times. In fact, I shared a cup of coffee with someone recently who indicated how surprised she is that there are so many people, including herself, who are really looking for some kind of fulfillment because they are so tired of being unfulfilled and uninterested in their own lives. She had always seen herself as an optimist and full of energy. Lately, however, she found that the temptation to just "give up" was becoming stronger.

The symptoms of burnout are very similar to the symptoms of depression, which are characterized by consistent and pervasive fatigue, a feeling of lethargy, a sense of emptiness, loneliness and a loss of joy. Sound familiar? People reaching a burnout stage rarely sleep well, or even after sleeping, feel tired.

Physical fatigue is not the only symptom. If burnout continues for a long period of time, victims are also more susceptible to all types and degrees of illness. Emotionally, they just don't care or want to bother about anything any more and tend to be irritable and generally dissatisfied with everything. Being in relationships is too much trouble, so they prefer to be left alone. Mentally, they can't concentrate, become forgetful, and find themselves uninterested in anything. These symptoms may lead to interpersonal, health, and performance problems, as well as substance abuse, and a sense that one's life is meaningless.

It is easy to become burned out in a world so full of uncertainty and overwhelming demands. We believe that no matter what we do, we can't seem to get control of our lives or renew our energy. This disorder is no respecter of persons. Young and old, men and women, rich and poor are becoming burned out in alarming numbers.

Burnout means that we've run out of energy. One way to visualize how the internal energy works is to use an analogy of a pot of fluid on the stove.

**Our energy often goes out faster than we can get it back in.**

**When our pot is full, we feel stress free and peaceful.**

**When our pot is only half full, we feel stressed.**

**When our energy is gone, we are burned out.**

**LIFE: It's often on HIGH!**

Our body is the pot, and the fluid is the internal energy in our bodies. Visualize this pot sitting on a burner called "life." From birth, every day whether we are awake or asleep, energy is going out of our pot. So the trick to being physically, emotionally, mentally and spiritually healthy is to continually put the energy back into the pot.

During the last 50 years, the heat of the burner just gets higher and higher because of the constancy of the stress cycle. So, the fluid, or our energy, evaporates from our pot more quickly than we can replenish it. Try as we might, our pots may only get half filled, at best. Many of us have lived or are living with our pots half full. And then, when a crisis hits or life throws a curve, we use all of our remaining energy and we experience burnout. If this empty pot continues to sit on the stove, the pot experiences melt-down. That's when we get sick, have major illnesses and, literally "burn out." When I look around today there are many people who are physically, emotionally and mentally exhausted. These are people who have no more energy, and only care about just getting through the day. Sometimes all we want to do is drop into bed, pull the covers over our head and hide.

Burnout doesn't happen all at once. It is a gradual, insidious process that devours all of our energy so that we have no more from which to draw. In fact, burnout happens in stages.

## STAGES OF BURNOUT

The burnout stages have no particular time frame and people can move between stages depending upon the circumstances. Once someone hits the wall, however, any chance of wholeness and health is practically hopeless. When we understand the stages of burnout, and the symptoms of each stage, we can guard against allowing the process to begin in our own lives.

### Honeymoon Stage
The honeymoon stage is aptly named because it is generally short-lived and very intense. It is characterized by an intense pressure to get many things done. We struggle with feeling guilty and doing all the "shoulds." There is a go, go, go, pressure-driven behavior that is difficult to calm down. While overachievers may be the most guilty of exhibiting this behavior, all of us are overloaded with the pressure to get things done. We all have so much to do because of the demands of our work, school, home and society. Why is it so hard to allow ourselves the few minutes

between tasks to "just do nothing?" I think, "I should check email." or "I should tackle a project, read a book or magazine." In other words, I feel guilty if I am not using absolutely every minute of the day in "productive activity." What is it that drives us to this frenetic behavior? Why do we find ourselves in the vicious cycle of having to DO so much?

It all starts from the time we are born until we are about two years old when we believe that we are the center of the universe. We believe that the only reason the universe exists is for our pleasure. We learn this because everyone in our universe is fussing over us, feeding us, loving us, throwing us in the air, tickling our tummies and kissing us. This is a very important period in our lives. In fact, there is a fatal disease afflicting babies from birth to six months old, which is caused when babies are not touched. When we are not touched and held, we die. We learn in the first two years of our lives that we are important, unique, special, lovable, adorable, perfect, gifted, deserving and everything wondrous. We know that we are loved and perfect simply because we exist.

And then, something dreadful happens when we turn two years old. We discover that our mommies and daddies were just kidding. Do you remember the two very important words you learned as a small child besides "mamma" and "daddy"? We learned "No" and "Don't." We learn that we are not loved just because we are. We learn that we are loved for what we do. If we do it right, then we will get the prize. Do you remember as a child: "If you do this... then you will get this ..."? For example, "If you clean your room, Mamma will give you a cookie." "If you get good grades in school, you'll get a good job." "If you are good husband or wife, you'll get to stay married and live happily ever after." "If you study your courses as hard as you can, and go to every one of your classes, then you will get an A in this course." "If you go to work on time, do everything the boss tells you to do, and are dependable, then you'll be able to keep your job."

Surprise!! All the rules have changed. Nothing is certain anymore. And all the things we think we have been doing right no longer count. That fact gets registered in the subconscious and our little "Polly Paranoid" who sits on our shoulder says to us,

"Aha! You are not doing enough. You need to be doing more things." That's when the negative cycle begins. In order to feel a sense of worthiness we believe we have to do more things. The honeymoon stage is trying to figure out how to do it "right" so that we can believe that we are competent and successful. That's why the honeymoon stage is so intense and so short-lived; because when you do more and more, you eventually run out of gas, or energy, which leads to the second stage of burnout.

### Fuel Shortage

In the process of doing so much to gain acceptance by what we have achieved, we finally run out of gas. At this point we begin to get confused and start asking "Why?" and "Why me?" We ask ourselves, "Why am I still so unhappy when I'm doing everything I can?" "How is it that I have all the material things I want, and I'm still not happy?" and "Where is the joy I'm supposed to have?" In our deeper levels, we become confused and hurt because we believe we are doing all that we can to gain acceptance. We begin to reason, "I know what the problem is, I'm not doing the right things." So, we set off to change geographical locations, change jobs, change relationships, spouses, houses, cars and anything else that will give us a temporary "hit" or "fix" to gain some sense of meaning. However, "nothing changes if nothing changes," and if we have not addressed the issues at our deeper levels, all of the superficial changes we make only provide a temporary high or fix, and then we are right back down in the black hole wondering why we have no joy. Only this time the hole is beginning to fill not only with confusion, but also with negativity, cynicism, resentment and anger. When the anger becomes pervasive, we have moved to the chronic stage of burnout.

### Chronic Stage

The Chronic stage of burnout is characterized by anger. When we are angry, it usually begins as a hurt to one of the major needs of the spirit—i.e. the need for self-esteem, security, competency, trust or love. When these needs continually are not met, energy is diminished and we end up not feeling hurt any longer. Instead we feel cynical, resentful or angry. Pervasive anger, whether it manifests as resentment, cynicism or depression, can be characteristic of burnout. We also have the misguided notion that when we are angry with someone or something, we are getting even with them. In fact, we are doing enormous damage to ourselves.

In order to understand the dynamics of hurt and anger and how these emotions are managed in women and men, let's use the analogy of the iceberg again. In considering the differences of acceptable behavior in this culture, look at the two represented icebergs below. One iceberg is labeled, "Men," and the other is labeled, "Women."

The visible part of the iceberg shows acceptable behavior for both men and women in this culture; what is below the surface,

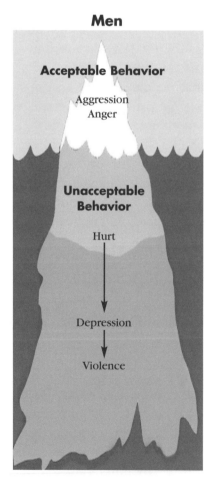

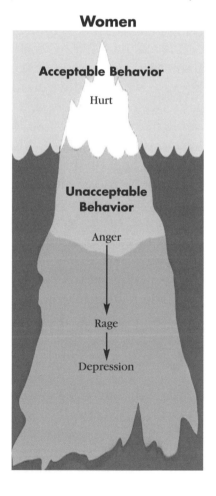

the invisible, is what is unacceptable behavior for both men and women. It is important to learn that when certain behaviors are accepted or not accepted in this culture, it can impact what we do, behaviorally, and how we handle the feelings associated with those behaviors.

In the Western culture, men, generally, are permitted to be aggressive and show their anger. When men are tough it is considered the highest compliment. These are the men who are the titans of business, government, law and many other professions. If we pay attention to the ads in the media, we will see men who sweat, swagger and swill. When men meet each other they often joust and tease by calling each other names. They slap each other on the back and verbally banter with each other. This kind of aggressive behavior is acceptable and expected. In fact, on TV it's considered funny and masculine.

It is also acceptable for men to show their anger. It is admirable when men are strong and tough. So at the tip of the "male" iceberg, men's aggressive and angry behavior is acceptable in this culture. However, men have a harder time dealing with hurt, which, when it becomes buried below the surface of the iceberg, becomes depression. It's okay for men to be angry, but it's not okay for them to feel hurt. So men suppress their hurt. Men don't normally admit that their feelings are hurt. Over a period of time when these feelings of hurt are not addressed, they manifest as depression. When depression is repressed for a long period of time, or not resolved, it finally may explode into violence.

Recently, there was a story of a very dedicated and bright man who had retired from a very successful career. He and his wife were admired in the community as the highest example of success in every way. His wife was found beaten to death with a blunt instrument and he hanged himself. What is sad about this story is that on the surface all of their friends believed them to be a very happy and adoring couple. It has been revealed since their deaths that he had been on medication for depression, and that he had tried to commit suicide before. It appears he was never able to quiet his internal demons.

In contrast to men and society's expectations, women, are permitted to say they are hurt. At the tip of their iceberg we find that it is more acceptable for women to show vulnerability, show their hurt, even cry. (Unless she is in the business world, or running for public office.) Even though we are more tolerant of differences in women's behavior, when a woman steps out of her traditional role of tender nurturer, it is often unnerving. What can women not say? The answer is everything which is indicated below the surface of the iceberg. It is not acceptable for women to say "I'm angry!" When a woman says she is angry, the response is usually, "Well bitch, bitch, bitch or it must be that time of the month again." Have you noticed that most of the time when women are angry it is attributed to some time of the month or period in her life? She is either pre-menstrual, post-menstrual, menstrual, or pre-menopausal, menopausal, or post-menopausal. This is because it is not acceptable for women to be angry. There must be something to blame for it.

It is commonly known that men have "periods" too. They also have fluctuations in their testosterone levels. Do you ever hear men talk about having PTS (Pre-testosterone Syndrome)? Do you ever hear men attribute mood swings to "that time of their life?" Instead, we generally romanticize it and call it a "mid-life crisis." As a woman, have you ever thought that being menopausal was romantic?

Because this anger is not acceptable, in time, a woman's suppressed anger can become rage. Rage is not necessarily displayed by throwing temper tantrums. You can observe a woman's rage in a variety of ways. Sometimes she will totally reject intimate relationships; sometimes she will ignore any traditional roles expected of her; or, sometimes she rebels to impositions on her with a very clear, cold message that says "don't even think about it."

A few years ago there was a couple in New York who appeared to have an idyllic life. The husband adored his wife and gave her everything she wanted. They were very comfortable with homes in New York, Europe and Miami. One day after 37 years of marriage, the wife walked up to her husband with two suitcases and said, "Good-bye." Everyone in the family was distraught. Obviously, the poor soul had taken leave of her senses, was menopausal, and needed a professional to talk some sense into her. She told the professional, "For 37 years I never had a first name. I was Mrs. So and So, So and So's wife, Honey, Darling, Sweetheart, Mom. No one ever thought I had a first name. No one ever thought I thought. And one day, I snapped!" That's rage!

If the rage is not managed appropriately, it can become depression. We hear more and more about new drugs that try to solve the dilemma by making everyone happy. The prediction is that the drug of choice in the 21st Century will be Prozac or similar medications, and that they will outsell aspirin!

This negative energy, characterized by the chronic stage, which can become pervasive in both men and women is not only damaging to our relationships with others in our personal and professional lives, but, more importantly, it is incredibly damaging to our internal well being. When we get stuck in the chronic stage of burnout the prolonged negativity and anger can cause a breakdown in our immune system. When this occurs, we get sick, and enter the crisis stage of burnout.

## Crisis Stage

The Crisis stage of burnout is characterized by physical illness. Most illness and accidents can be attributed to prolonged stress. The illnesses that occur in this stage may cause the loss of life, or serious debilitation. Many people who have suffered major illnesses and medical catastrophes have seriously re-evaluated their living habits in this stage. It can either jolt them to consider healthy alternatives in their lives, or catapult them to the last stage of burnout.

## Hitting the Wall

Hitting the Wall is the end of the line. It means that a person either commits suicide by using a gun, car, food, drink, drugs, violence, and other destructive means, or they drop out of life. Many times, if they do not kill themselves, these individuals drop out of the mainstream of life and may become street people or institutionalized. They usually destroy themselves in one way or another as it is very difficult to regain energy when someone has come this far.

# How Stress and Burnout Affect the Immune System

Even if we never come to the "Crisis Stage" or "Hit the Wall," regular daily stress and burnout can compromise our immune system. Scientific understanding of the immune system has revealed some very interesting information about how the impact of stress and burnout affects physical, emotional, spiritual and mental health.

The immune system is complex in the way it protects the body from disease and infection. Our lifestyles can have a direct impact on the kinds of chemicals we release that trigger harmful or helpful, as well as addictive, reactions in our bodies. When we are stressed, fearful or angry, we release chemicals that can be harmful to the body. Over time, these harmful chemicals can break down our immune system and we get sick.

Conversely, some of the chemical substances that are carried on the neurotransmitters are endorphins, the chemical which gives a natural sense of well-being and health to the body.

The most fascinating aspect of the body's release of these harmful chemicals is that they are highly addictive. In examining the fear and anger response, for example, we know people who seem to thrive on thrill-seeking behavior, or those who seem unable to help themselves when they get angry or enraged. Deeper examination into fear and anger reveals that thrill-seeking behavior is a means of stimulating a fear response. Notice how many people thrive on excitement and a thrill. How many of us take chances, whether in traffic, in sports, in business, or in relationships? How many of us wait until the last minute to accomplish a task because when you do it at the last minute your senses are more acute? How many of us put ourselves in situations where we might get hurt or even killed? Remember how we felt? Remember how every nerve in our body stood at attention? Remember how awake, how intense, how vitally alive we felt? Remember how intensely focused we were?

Remember the last time you were angry? Remember how much energy you had? Remember how acute your senses were? It is no wonder that some of us like this state of being. The increase in thrill-seeking behavior and the need for stimulation, as well as the increase in violence, demands much more research. Could it be that over time many people in the world have become addicted to the release of chemicals they manufacture within their own bodies and to which they are now held captive? Where does the spiral of needing more and more thrill stimulation end? How does one stop the anger before it becomes hostility and violence? Not only are these unfortunate people in trouble, but so are those with whom they interact and become the target of their violence. The tragedy in all of this is that these people believe that when they are angry and violent, they are getting even and causing others pain.

What we don't realize, however, is that over prolonged periods of time, the release of harmful chemicals will eventually break down our own immune systems, causing major illness, perhaps leading to death.

Steven King wrote an unusual book about medieval good and evil called, *The Eye Of The Dragon*. The evil wizard, Flagg, developed the most potent and deadly poison in the world. When initially swallowed, the individual would be filled with energy and apparent good will. Eventually, a putrid smell would emanate from the person indicating that the poison was consuming the person from the inside out. Soon, the individual would be completely devoured and would evaporate without a trace. The effects of anger and resentment on individuals have the same effect. Anger gets into the core of our being and begins to eat us up from the inside out until eventually we are totally consumed.

How we handle the anger and fear in our lives is our responsibility. (Chapter 5 will give some suggestions on how to manage fear and anger.) It is critical to remember that when we allow negative energy to live within our bodies, it will eventually consume us with a destructive poison. Fortunately, the release of good chemicals is also addictive, much more manageable and brings more positive results. These issues and many more will be discussed in Part II of this book.

At each stage of burnout, we may stop the madness and destruction to ourselves. Sometimes, we may try superficial means to renew our psychic energy like buying a new house, new car, getting a new job, etc. To stop the spiraling effects of burnout, however, we must do some serious introspection and reflection about what is going on within the deeper levels of our Self. Part II addresses the importance of balancing all areas of your life to enable you to gain internal harmony and wholeness.

*References:* McGugan, Peter. *Beating Burnout.* This book has lots of good techniques to manage burnout.

Pert, Candace. *Molecules of Emotion.* Wonderful book, scientific but very readable, on the interconnectedness of our physical, emotional, spirit and mind.

Williams, Redford, Williams, Virginia. *Anger Kills.* An excellent book describing how anger breaks down one's immune system and destroys physically.

PART II

# Eliminating the Stress
# Beginning the Healing

*The problem is...more basically: how to remain whole in the
midst of the distractions of life; how to remain balanced, no
matter what centrifugal forces tend to pull one off center;
how to remain strong, no matter what shocks come in at the
periphery and tend to crack the hub of the wheel.*
Anne Morrow

Before we embark on the next section of the book, find a
piece of paper and pencil and write down the answers to the
following three questions:

1. List the five most important people in your life: You can
   include all of your brothers and sisters in one lump. If you
   have many children, you can include them in one lump. You
   can also include animals.

2. List the five areas where you spend the most time: The car, the
   bedroom, the bathroom, the kitchen, the building where you
   work, the gym, the grocery store, school, etc.

3. If you were to die tonight, God forbid, what would be the five
   things you have not finished yet? Some things you might
   include are your hopes and dreams, places you haven't been, a
   business you haven't started, or a skill you haven't learned.

When you are finished writing your answers, please look at
your answer to your first question. Among the most important
people on your list, did you include yourself? Those of you who
did, Bravo! Those of you who did not, why not? Is it because you
just take it for granted that you are on the list? Yes, perhaps you

take yourself for granted! Is it because you think you might be viewed as selfish?

When I was working on my degree in Theology, I was amazed that in all of the major religions of the world there are several common themes. All religions demand repentance, obedience, and a command to love our neighbor as ourselves. I have often asked myself what does it mean to love ourselves in this context? It means that we are to take care of ourselves, nourish ourselves and be kind to ourselves. This feels dramatically opposed to what we have been taught. However, when we travel on an airplane, the flight attendant reminds us that when the oxygen mask falls out from the overhead compartment, we are required to put it on ourselves first. Why? Because we can't help anyone else if we're dead. When we are not taking care of ourselves, we may be leaving a burden to others who might have to take care of us. Many of the health care costs are a result of people who have not taken care of their bodies through not eating properly, toxic addictions, lack of exercise, and negativity and anger. That is not loving the other most important people on your list.

Moving next to the answer to question #2: You may notice that where you spend most of your time is not necessarily with the people who are the most important people on your list. If you are not on the list of important people, you may not be attending to your need to care for yourself by being in places, or with people, who are nurturing to you.

I suppose that one of the places where you spend the most time is your place of work. Often you will notice that the people who seem to occupy your thoughts the most, and most often in a negative way, are some of the people you work around. Sometimes you may have lengthy and brilliant conversations with them in your head where you really tell them a thing or two. That kind of obsession only hurts you. If you would not invite those people to your house to dinner or for the weekend, don't allow them squatters rights in your head. Replace those obsessive, negative thoughts with pleasant and positive thoughts.

Question #3 asks if you have started planning or working toward all of your hopes and dreams. I can just hear you wail at me: "Denny, I just barely have enough time to get to work, get home, get the family cared for and get to bed!" I understand this dilemma. But, it is time to begin to manage your time and your life by gaining a sense of control and balance—first by knowing what to do then learning the techniques of how to do it. In the following chapters several techniques are given to help bring healing and balance to those seven areas in your life. The purpose of considering each area separately is to allow you to consider the many complex components that make up who you are and what your stress triggers might be.

LEARNING TO BALANCE IS THE KEY

# HEALING THE PHYSICAL

## Physical Stress Reducers

*We are not a physical being having a spiritual experience,*
*we are a spiritual being having a physical experience.*
Wayne Dyer

Buckminster Fuller said that humankind is 1% visible and 99% invisible. That means that 1% is what we can see or experience in the physical world. Isn't it amazing how much time, attention and money we spend on that 1%? I don't know about you, but I do! I spend an incredible amount of energy on my physical existence and I have spent hundreds of dollars on creams just for my face. Even though it may be only 1% it houses the other 99% of who we are and must be maintained, especially with regards to our health.

There are several ways to effectively manage the stresses in our lives by paying attention to things we can do in the physical area. The most obvious is taking care of our body.

## LISTEN TO YOUR BODY

As I mentioned earlier, each of us has a finite amount of energy to expend each day. This is not just physical energy, but emotional, spiritual and intellectual energy as well. Our bodies have a way of signaling when things are right or wrong. We know when we feel sick, or need food and water. Our body also tells us when we need rest, exercise, and, also, when we have abused it. It is important that we learn to listen to our body and to know our limits.

### Physical Limits

There are only so many activities that we can tolerate at one time before our body tells us to stop. What are the signs that we are accustomed to ignoring? Do we seem to "catch every little bug that comes along," do we seem to tire more easily, are we more impatient and irritable, are we more forgetful, lightheaded, more constipated, or have upset stomachs more often? Our body may be warning us to slow down and pay attention to our physical needs because it only has so much energy with which to manage a variety of activities.

Believe it or not, one of the very important things to do for yourself is exercise. "Aaaccck—I don't have time!" you say. But the benefits of healthy exercise have been thoroughly document-ed. For years experts have told us that the speediest way to get good chemicals into your blood stream is through exercise.

To help your body to deal with stress and to prepare the body for stressful times, daily exercise is strongly recommended because every day the body takes in toxins which accelerate the destruction of healthy cells. We need oxygen fed into our blood stream to ensure healthy blood flow and the regeneration of good and healthy cells. In 1990, the American College of Sports Medicine (ACSM) updated its position statement on the quantity and quality of exercise recommended for maintaining fitness. For health's sake ACSM specifies that people should spend an accumulated minimum of 30 minutes in some sort of physical activity four to five days a week. The activity need not be sports related. Eight minutes spent climbing up stairs, another 10 spent pulling weeds, and 12 more spent walking the dog all contribute to the day's total.

The American Heart Association states that all of us should exercise at least four days a week, 1/2 hour each session. The 1/2 hour should include a five minute warm up and 20 minutes of hard exercise to increase your heart rate as recommended by the AHA. Any exercise is good for you as long as you maintain the proper heart rate for a steady 20 minutes.

I must emphasize here that it's not that physically active people don't get stressed. It's just that getting out and getting the body moving around helps to physically work out the stress. In my own life, I get plenty stressed. When I start feeling the fear and stress, getting out and exercising, even if it's a short walk, is enormously helpful. It doesn't bring me more business, doesn't reassure me that I am worthwhile, but it releases physical tension and releases good chemicals into my body, which helps me to face whatever lies ahead.

## Nutrition

*(A big "thank you" to my good friend Kathy Heyl, M.S., R.D., Chair, Department of Health Professionals, Assistant Professor of Nutrition, Metropolitan State College of Denver, for her contribution to this portion of this chapter.)*

Nutrition, also, plays a very important role in decreasing stress in your life. The old adage, "you are what you eat" still applies. When we get anxious and stressed, it's easy to head for the comfort food—chocolate, macaroni and cheese, potatoes and gravy, fried chicken and anything else that's fried or loaded with sugar. It is important that you eat fresh fruit, fresh vegetables, fiber and restrict how much fat you eat. You may ask "Why all the fuss over what I eat?" Every day we all take in our bodies toxic substances called "free radicals." These substances can be in the air we breathe, foods we eat, and substances we abuse. It is a little like taking rust into our bodies which breaks down the cells.

As you may know, all of our cells in our body die and are replenished. Some cells die more rapidly than others, but over a one-year period, all of the cells in the body are replenished with the exception of our brain cells and particular cells in the lung. When these cells die, it is important that new healthy ones take their place.

To ensure healthy cells are replenished, it is important that your body takes in anti-oxidants, foods with vitamin C and E, and foods with beta-carotene. These foods are:

- Fresh dark green leafy vegetables, squash, carrots, tomatoes, green and red peppers, broccoli and other vegetables that are dark green, orange or red.
- Fresh fruits with beta-carotene are cantaloupe, dark red berries, (blueberries, blackberries, raspberries, dark red grapes), mangoes, peaches and apricots.

If we eat at least a fresh salad every day and two fresh fruits, that will certainly help to get our daily requirement of beta carotenes.

It is very important that we:

- Drink at least two quarts of clear water a day. It is the only substance we take into our body that is hydrating, not de-hydrating. It is much harder to slough off dead cells and keep the body lubricated and healthy without filling it with fresh water.
- Keep our colon clean and regular. Water and foods with fiber will help. The purpose here is to keep toxins out of our body, and replenish the dying cells with healthy new ones. This helps fight disease as well as aging.

There are several substances that, when eaten, tend to mimic or trigger the stress response. Likewise, stress can deplete your body of the necessary nutrients, vitamins, and minerals. Here are some examples:

1. *Sugar.* Excess amounts of simple sugars (found in regular soda pop, candy, etc.) tend to displace vitamins, particularly the B-complex vitamins (niacin, thiamin, riboflavin, and B-12). When the B-complex vitamins are lacking, you might experience fatigue, anxiety, and irritability. In addition, eating large amounts of simple sugars can cause big fluctuations in your blood glucose levels, resulting in pronounced fatigue, headaches and general irritability.
2. *Caffeine.* Food sources with caffeine trigger the stress response, specifically an increased heart rate. The result is a heightened state of alertness that makes the individual more susceptible to perceived stress. Caffeine can be found in many foods, including chocolate, coffee, tea, and several beverages.

3. *Salt.* High sodium intake from salt is associated with high blood pressure because sodium acts to increase water retention. As water volume increases in a closed system, blood pressure increases. If this condition persists, it may contribute to hypertension.

4. *Vitamin and mineral deficiency.* Chronic stress can cause a depletion of water-soluble vitamins (B and C) that are necessary for energy metabolism. Stress can also deplete calcium stores in the body and prevent the absorption of calcium in bone tissue.

The American Dietetic Association issued a press release recently indicating that if you are mentally or emotionally stressed out, these few eating tips may help:

1. Don't binge, or just grab whatever is in sight—take time for eating.
2. Try quick foods and recipes using fresh, canned or frozen veggies and fruits. Order in if you have to, but try not to skip meals.
3. Take time out for a healthy breakfast before your day starts. It will get you going for your busy day.

*Recommendations for healthy eating habits*

The Cleveland Clinic recommends the following guidelines for healthy eating to fight stress:

- Eat a wide variety of healthy foods—well balanced amounts of carbohydrates, fats, fiber and proteins.
- Eat in moderation—control the portions of the foods you eat.
- Reach a healthy weight and maintain it.
- Eat at least 5 to 9 servings of fruits and vegetables per day.
- Eat food that is high in dietary fiber such as whole grain cereals, legumes and vegetables.
- Minimize your daily fat intake. Choose foods low in saturated fat and cholesterol.
- Limit your consumption of sugar and salt.
- Limit the amount of alcohol that you drink.
- Make small changes in your diet over time.

- Combine healthy eating habits with a regular exercise program.

All nutritionists seem to agree that:

1. It's important to eat a good breakfast, and space meals evenly throughout the day. This allows a constant energy source to be available to the body in a consistent flow. When one or two large meals are consumed, so much digestive energy is involved to process the food that it detracts from the energy needed for alertness throughout the day.
2. Avoid or minimize the consumption of caffeine, sugar, salt and alcohol.
3. Eat a diet that provides a balance of all of the food groups.
4. Eat lots of fruits and vegetables.

### Natural Healing Remedies

More and more people are discovering the benefits of natural herbs and alternative medical remedies for a variety of minor illnesses and for maintaining health. Recommended reading in these areas is included at the end of this chapter.

### Relaxation Breaks

Whenever I am involved in any intense type of task, I find it is helpful to take a short little relaxation break often. These breaks help relieve tensions that have been built up in my musculature. If allowed to remain tense, our muscles can become sore and pinched causing more serious maladies. A short break is about four or five minutes of changing my position, getting a glass of water, stretching my muscles and looking at something else. Longer breaks, around 15 minutes, can be taken alone where we can get off by ourselves and breathe deeply, listen to music, or hum a favorite tune. These breaks need not be lengthy. It's just important to find some way to distract ourselves from the task at hand for a few moments. It is important during these little mini-breaks that we are totally distracted from the present task and breathe deeply. Sometimes taking four or five deep sighs will help.

## Rest and Sleep

A sure sign my body is tired is when I get weepy and emotional. One of the fastest ways to burn ourselves out is not to get enough sleep. It is important that we honor our body's request for however much sleep it needs. If, however, we sleep consistently more than nine hours a day, it may be a sign that we are depressed, and in that case, we need to see a doctor. An easy test to determine whether we are burning out is the "T-T" test—i.e. "Testy and Tired."

Most researchers agree that we sleep in about 90 minute sleep cycles. Sometimes the cycles may be less, sometimes more, but generally they are about 1 1/2 hours. There are a lot of important things that happen in those cycles and researchers believe we need at least five sleep cycles a night, which is about 7 1/2 hours of sleep. The first part of the cycle is deep sleep whereby we heal our physical self, the second part of the cycle is REM (rapid eye movement) or the dreaming portion that heals our spirit needs and the third part is the transition of coming out of the dreaming, or dozing phase and then moving back into the next cycle again.

If you have been working hard physically, you may find that the deep sleep portion of your sleep cycle is longer. If you are going through a change, are troubled about events in your life and you find yourself dreaming a great deal, you might have longer REM periods. If you are struggling with worry or fears about issues at work, with family or in your personal life you may feel that you have been dozing all night. Because of the long dozing period, you may believe you have not slept all night.

To help understand sleep cycles and how they impact our body, let's assume that you have gone to sleep at 10 p.m. and have set your alarm for 5 a.m. At 4 a.m. you wake up and think to yourself, "I feel pretty good—I'm awake!" (You have theoretically finished 4 sleep cycles) You look at the clock and it is 4 a.m. and you say to yourself, "It's only 4 a.m. I'm not getting up now." So you go back to sleep and when the alarm goes off at 5 a.m. how do you feel? Most of us feel like a truck has run over us. Why? Because we didn't finish the sleep cycle. So if you wake up at 4 a.m. and you're awake, get up and make up the extra sleep cycle either the next night or later in the week. Researchers also tell us that we only need one extra sleep cycle to make up for loss of sleep within our own circadian rhythm cycle. (Your body rhythms in terms of sleep and metabolism.) Try it. You'll find that when you begin to be aware of your sleep cycles and pay attention to them you will feel better during the day.

Power napping is another major source of gaining some needed energy. Some researchers have indicated that 20 minutes is the optimum amount of sleep for a power nap. If you go any longer your body may be fooled into thinking you get to go into the deep sleep portion of your cycle and then you feel all groggy when you wake up. If you can't get a full 90 minutes for a nap, then settle for a power nap which would be 20 minutes or less.

To learn to power nap is easy. Get an egg timer, a blanket, pillow, your woobie and curl up comfortably. It takes practice, but don't worry. The egg timer will wake you up. Sometimes when you come home from work, all you need is just a few minutes to doze to re-energize yourself. Make a deal with other household members to give you just a few minutes to re-energize.

## SELF CARE—GIVING YOURSELF GIFTS

Giving ourselves a gift every day affirms that we are important and worthwhile. Why is this so important? As we saw earlier, we forget about ourselves being on the list of the most important people in our lives. When we are not paying attention to ourselves, stress can sneak up on us very easily. One way to guarantee that we will remember how critical it is to take care of ourselves is to give ourselves a present every day. It doesn't matter how we describe the gift as long as we say to ourselves, "This is my present to me." For example, sometimes while I'm waiting for someone, I will read a magazine I don't normally have time to read, or put my head back in the chair, close my eyes and just take deep breaths. This little "mini-break" is a present to me. If you find yourself with a few minutes to yourself every day, say to yourself, "This is a little 'mini break,' my present to me." And use it as a time to escape into reflection, quiet, reading, or whatever pleases you.

We can buy ourselves something or give ourselves a gift that costs nothing, like taking a walk, reading a book, watching a favorite movie, or having a nice bubble bath. We just need to say to ourselves each time: "This is my present to me." These "presents" can be rituals that give you pleasure. For example, I always look forward to Friday night so I can watch a good movie or read a good book. By continually remembering to give something tangible to ourselves, we may begin to remember to pay attention to how we care for ourselves in other ways. This attention to ourselves helps give us the sense that we are in control of ourselves, therefore it helps to ward off the stress reaction.

### Gifts of Time

It's no news that all of us want more time. Let me share with you a little secret about time that has been helpful to me in reducing stress over the years. We don't have to do every project on our list all at once. Projects like cleaning the garage, cleaning the drawers, organizing pictures, or cleaning the files on the computer can be done in smaller segments. The reason why this book has taken me so long to write is because I kept thinking I had to spend long periods of time just writing. It was always so hard to find either one day or three or four hours to set aside for "writing the book." Weeks would roll by and I had not taken the time to write. Then I realized that I could spend a one-hour block of time, rather than a four or five-hour block of time, and the book finally got finished. I have discovered that in all of my projects, it has helped to give me a sense of accomplishment and has reduced my stress enormously when I don't try to finish the whole project at once.

Remember the five things you haven't finished yet? Take a one-hour segment every week to start on one of those projects. Maybe it is reading an educational book that will contribute to a new career. Maybe you want to learn a new language. You might spend 1/2 an hour every day or three days a week listening to a language tape. Maybe you want to learn a musical instrument. You might spend one hour three days a week practicing. Maybe you want to start a new business. You can set out a timeline and a step-by-step process to learn everything you need to know about starting that particular business. Maybe you want to start a new career. You can take one course at a time that will contribute to your credentials to begin that career.

Whatever dreams you have twirling around inside your heart, begin now to give yourself the gift of time, in smaller segments, each week to advance the fulfillment of those dreams.

### *Special Gifts*

Some ideas for giving ourselves gifts are:

- Taking a Saturday or Sunday morning drive by ourselves or with someone we love.
- Taking time to go for a walk or play our favorite game.
- Take an hour or two hours every week to do exactly what we want to do.
- Spend an evening with that significant other watching a favorite movie.
- Take a 20 minute bubble bath.
- Send ourselves a special card and sign it "from your secret admirer." (It not only will give us a lift, it will drive everyone at work crazy wondering who the secret admirer is.)
- Bring flowers or a plant for our work area.
- Buy special bath and body products.
- Save a certain amount of money each week for that really big purchase we want. Every time we put that money in our jar or box, make sure we say, "this is for my present to me."
- Buy that gadget we've wanted whether it is really useful or not.

The trick is that we have to say every time we do this, "This is my present to me." After a period of time, we will begin to notice that we are paying more attention to ourselves and our own needs. When this happens we are on the road to taking better care of ourselves.

## Live in the Present

It has been said that 87% of our thoughts are negative and 82% of those thoughts are on future or past events. Most of our time is spent thinking or obsessing about future events that haven't happened yet, or past events that we now have no control over. While obsessing we miss the wonderful moments right in front of us. There are many stories of people who have had near death experiences, significant emotional events, major illnesses, who recount that the greatest lesson they learned from these experiences was how precious living and enjoying each day is. It is hard to worry when we're involved in the present, because we can't worry when we are engrossed. As long as we live totally in the present moment, we are fully focused. No matter how stressed, anxious, panicked or afraid I am, I find that if I focus on the something right in front of me, it helps me to calm myself. One of my closest friends lives alone and when she gets distressed, anxious or angry, she cooks. Many times she will invite friends over to share the tasty results of her distress!

Part of living in the present is being mindful and focused in the moment we are living. It requires being fully aware of ourselves and our surroundings. Are we aware of our body, our emotions, our senses, the colors and sounds around us? Are we thinking about how we are feeling in the midst of the moment? Or, are we distracted and preoccupied so that by the end of the day we don't remember many of the events that have occurred? Do we only have a recollection of one or two things that may have been positive to us throughout the day?

Being mindful means paying close attention to the moment we are presently in. While we are eating, for example, do we watch television, or read the paper? Do we stop and think about the food, how good it tastes, the color, the texture, the people who picked or prepared it? Are we aware of our own body while we eat? While we talk are we thinking about the meanings of what we are saying? Are we aware of the other person with whom we are talking? What are they saying, how are they saying it, what do they really look like? These are important ways to be mindful in the moment. Being mindful means that we pay attention to everything around us and how we interact with our environment at every moment. It is hard to be worried or preoccupied when we are so involved and engrossed in the moment. The next time you are fully engrossed in the moment, be aware of how much at peace and contented you are.

## Get Busy

I have been teased all of my life about how I obsess about things, especially when I fantasize the worst possible outcomes. When this happens I not only get caught in devastating emotional trauma, but I also have a tremendous adverse physical reaction. I have learned over the years that when I am busy, I am distracted from my worries, troubles and stresses. It is part of living in the present. When I'm busy and attentive, it becomes easier to become absorbed and forget about the stressors.

I had some very dear older friends who struggled with so many of life's problems—their children, their health, their safety. In spite of those fears, every day they would get up and make their list of what had to be done that day, eat their breakfast and read the paper from cover to cover. It was that every day list of activities that kept them vibrant, interesting and alive well up into their 90's.

The most common manifestation of burnout is the total lack of interest in doing any physical activity. Sometimes the emotional and spiritual fatigue is so intense that it affects one's physical energy, as well. Whenever we feel that we absolutely cannot go on another minute, that we cannot get out of bed or perform one task, we can, at least, try to accomplish just one thing. That one thing may be just getting out of bed, or taking a shower, or fixing something to eat for ourselves. It's the little steps that contribute to self-esteem: the step-by-step process of moving through the tasks that make up our lives.

The act of being absorbed and involved gives our minds and psyches time to rest. Sometimes that little bit of extra time will be just enough to help us move past the anxiety and stress to realize that the issue that is troubling us is manageable after all. It also may be enough time to allow ourselves to come up with a solution.

## CUT OUT ACTIVITIES AND PRIORITIZE WHEN STRETCHED

For whatever reason, many of us are overachievers. We usually want to do it all and have it all. Or, situations often force us to accomplish several tasks and projects at the same time. If we are raising small children who need our care and attention, going to school to gain a degree, taking on special projects at work, and/or volunteering for school projects or involved in other volunteer organizations, we need to stop and ask ourselves if trying to do it all and all at once is making us unnecessarily stressed. Why are we in such a hurry? If we are working on additional educational degrees, but have high parental demands, we might want to take fewer hours per quarter. If we have a demanding schedule at

 work or school, relinquish activities that may be demanding more time and energy than we have to give until such time as we are able to take on more tasks. If we are in the midst of a major transition such as a divorce, marriage, death of a close loved one, having a baby, moving, graduating, or any other transitional change in our lives, it will help to reduce stress if we let go of extracurricular activities in order to manage our finite resources of energy.

# WARM UP SLOWLY

Statistics have shown that most heart attacks occur in the morning and most of those occur on Monday mornings. Because we like to postpone the inevitable, we wait to the last minute to get going in the morning and then find ourselves rushed, creating tension and anxiety. Getting up slowly gives us time to warm up to the day. I know people who can bounce out of bed and twitter and chirp through the morning. Others of us are slugs and it takes more time. Sometimes it may be setting the snooze alarm to allow five or ten more minutes to get up. It may be an extra two minutes in the shower with hot water on the back of our neck. It may be staring out the window while we wait for the coffee or tea to be ready. Whatever it is, allowing ourselves a few minutes to "get going" helps so we don't feel rushed and tense. Many people stop on the way to work or school to have breakfast, read the paper, or visit with friends. Some wait until they get to work and find a quiet spot to gear up for the day. It's amazing how those few minutes can set us up for a calmer day because we feel we have more control of ourselves.

# SURROUND YOURSELF WITH PLEASANTNESS

Another important principle to relieve stress is to surround ourselves with pleasant people and things. Many have the mistaken belief that "if there is no pain, there is no gain." In other words, if one is not suffering, then one is not getting the full benefit or learning from the situation. I can promise every one of you that before you die, you will suffer. Before we die, everyone of us will cry, be sad, hurt and be close to despair. Why then, do we want to go looking for it? I promise that suffering will find us soon enough. So it is important to bring as much pleasantness as possible into our lives. There are many ways to do this.

## Surround Yourself with Pleasant People

There are many troubled people in the world who are uncomfortable to be around. The negative energy that is released can only be harmful to us. So we need to get away from them. Sometimes this is not easy to do, particularly if we work or live with them. It is important for us to remember that when someone is unpleasant, it is about them, not us. I'm not implying that this is easy. But we cannot be responsible for another's happiness. It is important to move away from their negative energy by either physically removing ourselves from their presence as often as we can, or doing our best to understand them and try to forgive them for their unkindness. By forgiving them, we don't allow the negative energy to control us.

Over the years, I have heard hundreds of stories about people who live with difficult spouses, work with difficult people and have to put up with difficult relatives and children. If we are confronted with someone who is difficult or unpleasant, it is particularly necessary for us to find a place that can be called our sanctuary out of their presence. If we find ourselves consistently dreading to go home or to work because of having to be in this person's presence, we must find ways to stop the feeling of dread either through making steps to get out of the relationship, or find a way to bear it by creating a place of solace for ourselves, a peaceful place where we feel safe. Make that area as pleasant as possible by surrounding it with books you enjoy, pictures that are meaningful and music that is soothing.

It's also helpful to create a pleasant surrounding in our car or truck. If we put the things we like around us to remind us of what's important or what is comforting to us, when we become stressed or agitated in our vehicle, we can turn on music or a book on tape that we enjoy, or a comedy tape to help us laugh. The point is to keep pleasantness around us in order to relieve whatever the stress is in that moment.

# ORGANIZE

Another major stress producer is feeling we have no control over our time and/or being unorganized. Have you noticed that when you organize your "stuff" you feel better? My oldest daughter, Renny, has always been the one in the family who needs structure and likes to plan ahead. Her stress comes when she is caught off guard because something might occur that she did not plan. Renny is always on time, and is incredibly dependable because she organizes her life as best she can. Planning ahead, and organizing her life and calendar, have helped her to feel some sense of control over herself when there are so many other things in her life that are stressful.

Over the years I have learned many organizing tricks from people—some I have even incorporated into my own life. In the process of organizing our lives, it's important that we begin by making lists. When I talk to groups and individuals about making lists, they usually roll their eyes and say, "you're just adding to my stress!" Let me just remind you, again, that much of the time the reason why we get stressed is because we are trying to accomplish too many things with too little time. We feel out of control because we can't get everything done. Remember—one of the reasons why we get stressed is because we are overwhelmed. So...in order to manage that overwhelmed feeling, it's helpful to make lists.

## Making Lists

Many times we think of things to do when we are in the midst of some other activity where there is no accessible paper around to write a note. Make paper or post-it notes and pencils accessible in the most inhabited rooms of the house or car, and then every time you think of something else you need to do, while getting ready for work or school, driving in the car, watching television, reading a book, or whatever activity you are engaged in, you will be able to immediately write it down.

I make a master "to do" list. I start off with this master "to do" list the first of January and update it as I go along. I just let my mind free associate and write down all the things I want to accomplish. Then I separate it between personal and business things to do. At the beginning of each month, I write down things that need to be done that month, then further break it down week by week. If that seems too cumbersome, use whatever system will work best for you. I also like to use different colored pens or pencils to categorize work tasks: "have to dos," "later to dos," or "dreams." Even though I will not be able to finish everything on my list, just knowing it is written down is somehow comforting to me and serves as a reminder of what I hope to accomplish. It makes me feel that I'm in control. For example, if I have to renew my driver's license this year, I put it on my list. The deadline may be six months from now, but because it's on my list, it will trigger a mental reminder when I'm driving past the renewal agency so I can take a few minutes to accomplish the task. When items are on my list, it serves as a helpful reminder when opportunities arise to accomplish them.

I pull out the absolutely have-to-do's for each day from my weekly/daily "To Do" list. I either put those important tasks in my Daytimer or write them on a post-it note and put it someplace where I can refer to it often during the day.

I then use my crossed-off list to congratulate myself when each item is completed.

### Organizing Our "Stuff"

There are two major areas that need organizing—our "stuff" and our time. When I moved to my new home, in spite of the stress of moving, the joy of organizing my "stuff" was exhilarating. I cleaned closets, drawers, garage, basement, files—everything. Wow! It was great! I threw things away, gave things to Goodwill, and essentially felt purged when it was all over. In my case, I did it all at once, but you don't have to do it that way. Take one drawer at a time, one closet at a time or one room at a time. You know how good it feels.

When we spend a little time each month cleaning out closets, cupboards, and our garage it can be made more fun by watching movies or listening to our favorite music. Keep large plastic bags handy to periodically put in all of the things you don't want.

Then when the bags are full they are ready to go to the Salvation Army or Goodwill.

There is nothing more frustrating to me than having to take something back to the store because it doesn't work or doesn't fit. And these days we must have a receipt. So, for appliances or equipment, I find it helpful to put the receipt to my purchases with the warranties and directions so that if the item needs to be returned, it is where I can find it.

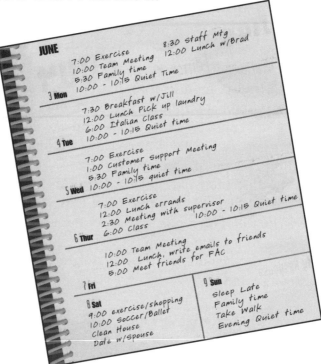

### Organizing Our Time

I have found that if I really use my calendar or time management system well, it helps me to organize my time and activities better. There are a lot of ways and things to organize. What works best for you? When we reflect on what and who our real priorities are, we then can make sure to schedule those priorities in our calendar every week—our exercise sessions, doing something for ourselves to help us grow and learn, spending time with our significant other, being ALONE, and time with our family or loved ones.

While we are updating our calendars for our business activities, it is also important that we keep track of personal activities. At first it may seem tedious, but don't give up. If we spend 15 to 20 minutes every Friday or Sunday to schedule our calendar for the following week, it will make a big difference in feeling that we have things more in control in our lives. And, once again, we know that one secret to managing stress is feeling we are in control.

## HAVE BACKUPS AND OPTIONS

In this frenzied life, our plans often become derailed. This can be a very simple problem of running out of bread, or as serious as losing one's job or a loved one. Have you planned ahead for life's many inconveniences and tragedies?

We can all tell stories of some of our most anxious and stressful moments when something has broken or we lose something right at the time when it is needed most. Where are the extra keys to our house, car and all of our locks? If our car breaks down, do we have another way to get to work? If our day-care provider falls through, do we have a back up?

Do we also have a back-up plan in case we change jobs? What are we doing to keep all of our options open to find ways to support ourselves? Do we have a back-up plan in case we cannot do what we do now?

In all areas of our lives, it is important that we have alternate plans in case our primary plans fall through.

## ASK: WILL THIS SIMPLIFY OR COMPLICATE MY LIFE?

All of us are confronted every day with decisions that must be made. Some of those decisions are very simple with few repercussions, while others might create complications. Whenever I am about to make any major decision in my life, I ask myself: "Will this decision simplify or complicate my life?" Sometimes the decision might make things complicated in the immediate future, but simplify my life later on. For example, when I bought a new house recently, it caused stress and anxiety in the immediate future while I attempted to budget for it, but in the long term, it will provide a source of comfort and investment for me. Taking a class toward a career goal may complicate your life now, but in the long term may help to give you more options toward your security. In all of our many decisions each day, it's helpful to quickly make a mental note to ask ourselves if our lives will become simpler or more complicated with the decision.

## Escape!

When I am feeling particularly stressed, the first thing I want to do is escape. But I have all of these "tapes" in my mind that tell me that I'm not facing up to my problems. Oh posh! It's impor-

tant to have ways to escape. There are a lot of things out there to help me—some good and some not so good. We may believe that drugs and alcohol are helpful for immediate relief, but in the long run they do immeasurable damage. But at times I still need to run away (or escape) even if it's just for a little while. So I do. I escape into a good book, a favorite movie or play, or dinner with friends.

Besides the daily gifts we give ourselves, we all need something special to look forward to. Of course, taking a vacation to someplace special or doing something we really enjoy can help in getting away and escaping. I also find it's helpful to take little mini-vacations throughout the year by finding as many opportunities as I can to interject a one or two-day vacation in my life.

## Playing

Playing is so important that a good friend of mine, Barbara Brannen, has dedicated her life to teaching people how to do it. Playing is doing something for no other reason than the sheer pleasure of doing it. It usually involves active participation rather than passive entertainment. When I watch children at play, I notice that not only do they become intensely involved and absorbed in the activity, but do so for long periods of time. Once I watched a friend's children take blankets and chairs to make a very elaborate fort. I was amazed that it wasn't just the end result of having a completed fort that was so important, it was the building of it. I know that it is this absorption that is healing because it lifts us from the worry, stress and anxiety to a total focus on the present moment. It was noted earlier that it is important to surround ourselves with pleasant things. It is also important to do fun things. Do we know how to play, whether it is a game, being goofy, clowning around, hanging out with friends, or playing with children or animals? The purpose of play is to have no other purpose than to play and enjoy the moment.

## Surround Yourself with Music

The first thing that happened as the Taliban was finally removed in Afghanistan was the playing of music. When I heard the news I was touched and impressed. We all want and need music in our lives. From the beginning of time we have had some type of music to express the deep emotions of the spirit. Humming, singing and listening are ways of responding to the deep joy or pain within us. Music is a great healer because it can capture all the diverse moods and express them in a way that touches us. The magic of music helps us to express the thoughts and feelings that are hard for us to put into conventional language.

So, whenever we're stressed, anxious, worried, angry, tired, bored, burned out, or depressed—whatever the emotion happens to be—listening to music will helps us express that emotion in a healing way.

# Massage Therapy

One of the most powerful ways to heal the body and mind and relieve stress is through message therapy. I have a friend who lost his wife recently to breast cancer. He spent many weeks caring for her until she died. One morning after the funeral, he could hardly get out of bed because of so many tight muscles in his back and neck. He finally broke down and went to a massage therapist. When he self-consciously lay down on her table, he jumped at her first touch. He told me that when he felt her hands massaging his muscles he realized that he had not been touched for months and he began to weep. The therapist understood and continued to work on him until he was finally relieved and relaxed.

We need to be touched. Kind, loving touch is therapeutic. We need to work out our muscle tension. Massage therapy has become a requirement in many people's lives because they have found that it is absolutely necessary to relieve stress. If money is an issue, find a massage school in your area. Better yet, make a deal with your partner to give each other massages at least once a week. (It is most helpful if you don't give each other massages on the same night. The one who goes first may not get the full benefit of the massage.) Using special massage oils with relaxing aromas can be very soothing and totally relaxing.

# Rituals

Rituals are a very important part of all of our lives. We have engagement rituals, weddings, funerals, church, graduation—almost everything in life has a ritual attached. Have we ever asked ourselves why they are so important? Rituals signify a transition—moving from one state to another. Personally, I think we need a daily ritual to symbolize moving from work to personal time. It is helpful to have a very simple physical ritual to make the statement to ourselves that we are moving from one transition to another. For example, when we are finished with our work day, we could have our slippers in our car to change into, or something else that helps us to physically "remove" work from us, and move into our own personal place.

A possible transition is that when you get home from work, always change your clothes even if you have been able to wear casual wear to work. If you like to take a walk after work, read the paper, take a power nap, whatever activity you do, use it as a method to move from one segment of your life to another.

In the morning while getting ready for your day, do not start obsessing or thinking about the day's events. Instead, use the car or transportation to work as the transition time to plan your day's activities. It's important that we zealously guard our personal time and keep it as separate as we possibly can from all other areas of our lives.

Another reason for the importance of everyday rituals in our lives is that it brings a sense of stability, control and consistency. In the world and in our personal lives where so much is changing at an incredible rate of speed, it is helpful to feel in charge of ourselves by at least having certain things we do every day giving us the sense of control over our own lives.

I have shared some ideas with you about caring for yourself physically that have worked for me and others. You probably have other great ideas. I encourage you to write them down and keep them handy to remind you when you are in the midst of a stressful situation. Pick out one or two ideas from this chapter that you will begin to do. Write them down on a post-it note and put it someplace where you will see it every day. The idea is to manage the stresses in your life by taking control and being mindful of the physical area of your Self. Even doing one of these activities will help you gain control of your life and help to relieve the stress.

**References:** Seaward, Brian Luke. *Managing Stress: Principles and Strategies for Health and Well Being.* I have repeated this reference because Luke has so many good ideas about how to manage your physical well being in order to manage stress.

Borbely, Alexander. *Secrets of Sleep.* This is a very comprehensive book about sleep and very readable.

Enright, James Thomas. *The Timing of Sleep and Wakefulness.* Another good book about sleep and sleep disorders.

Weissbluth, Marc. *Healthy Sleep Habits, Happy Child.* Even though this book sounds like it is only about children, it has wonderful insights into all aspects of sleeping for both children and adults.

Brannen, Barbara. *The Gift of Play.*

Heinerman, John. *Heinerman's New Encyclopedia of Fruits and Vegetables.*

Maky, Richard. *The New Age Herbalist.*

*Business Week,* January 2004, Cover Story, *"I Can't Sleep."*

# HEALING THE EMOTIONS
## Emotional Stress Reducers

*If you are losing a tug-of-war with a tiger, give him the rope
before he gets to your arm. You can always buy a new rope.*
Max Gunther

*Whining is a great deal of self pity pushed through a small hole.*
Anonymous

Scientists tell us that we are feeling animals who have learned
how to think, and it's the way we think and believe about things
that causes our feelings to go the way they do.

Our minds are powerful. Hamlet said, "...There is nothing
either good or bad, but thinking makes it so." Have you noticed
that sometimes within the same circumstance you can feel totally
different emotions? Whatever it is we are experiencing can have a
negative or positive impact sometimes within minutes of each
other. I can be having dinner with my family and feel overwhelming loving and warm feelings and within minutes feel melancholy
because I don't have a man in my life who could be sitting at the
table enjoying this wonderful family with me. This kind of see-
sawing goes on all the time.

Just as we have nerve endings in our body to alert us to physical pain, we also have nerve endings to our spirit to alert us to
psychic pain. Our emotions are the nerve endings to our spirit.
When the spirit has been damaged in any way, the emotions send
up red flags to tell us that we hurt. Emotions don't, however, tell
us what need is missing. We only sense anxiety, hurt, fear, anger, or
pain. When the basic needs of positive self-esteem, security, competency, trust and love are not met, the following sequence of
steps toward anger occurs.

FEAR OF UNMET SPIRIT NEEDS

UNMET NEEDS LEAD TO HURT

CONFUSION RESULTS

CREATES NEGATIVITY

Leads to CYNICISM, RESENTMENT and

DEPRESSION ◀ ANGER ▶ ACTING OUT
SUICIDE HOSTILITY/VIOLENCE

The anger spiral begins when we are afraid or perceive that our spirit needs will not be met; these hurt feelings create a sense of confusion. Often people ask themselves, "Why me? I've done everything I was supposed to do. I've been a good person. I can't understand why this is happening to me." If there is no resolution to this confusion, the next step down the cycle is negativity.

Negativity exhibits itself in complaining and criticism. One may be pessimistic or always find something negative in every situation rather than looking for things that are positive and affirming. If this negativity continues, it then leads to cynicism.

Cynicism is characterized by sharp criticisms, doubts and suspicions of others and their motives. Cynicism is usually directed toward a group of people because one or more people within that group have disappointed you. For example, if you are a woman and have had negative relationships with men, you may determine that all men are worthless. The same is true of men who have had negative relationships with women. He then might distrust, dislike and criticize all women. Cynicism can be directed to men, women, politicians, government agencies, young people, older people, etc.

If we allow the cynicism to become a part of us, it will eventually lead to anger. Anger can reveal itself in two extreme ways. One may act out by becoming extremely hostile and violent, or, at the other extreme, become very withdrawn, isolated, insular, or depressed. If one allows oneself to become cynical, angry, hostile or withdrawn, it can take an enormous emotional and physical toll. It is critical, therefore, to learn to intervene quickly to relieve the suffering caused by these very negative emotions.

## PERSONALITY TYPES AND INTERPERSONAL CONFLICT

All of us have an arrangement of characteristics or traits that make up a personality type. Many personality theorists have spent their lifetimes studying how our personalities shape the way we view circumstances and function in life. Sometimes personalities in people are so opposite that it causes friction in relationships and becomes a personality conflict. Being in a relationship with someone with a very different personality from our own can be very stressful.

There are many instruments to help us understand our personality type. I encourage you to find one not because I think we need labels, but because it helps us to understand how we relate to others and how to help ourselves in our relationships. The two I am most familiar with are the MBTI, commonly known as the Myers Briggs, and the Social Styles Inventory (Merrill, David, Reid, Roger. Personal Styles and Effective Performance).

## WRITING THINGS DOWN

If our emotions are like nerve endings which are feeling pain, the way to heal the pain is to find a healthy way to release the emotions. Medical and mental health professionals know how impor-

tant it is to work out issues that are troubling the mind in a physical way. Writing things down on paper through journaling or on a pad of paper, in the opinion of many counselors and therapists, is one of the most healing activities any of us can do for ourselves. One very beneficial way to release the pent-up chaos of our emotions is to remove them from our mind and put them on paper. It is the movement from the mind to paper, and the ability to examine the words in front of us, that creates a kind of objectivity which brings clarity and understanding.

Writing things down is only effective when we make sure that we are writing for our eyes only. It is important to keep writing and writing until we have run out of things to write. If we want to save it to read at a later time, we need to make sure to put the writing away where it absolutely cannot be seen by anyone else, because when we write for someone else, we are not really getting to the truth that lies within ourselves. It is safer to tear our papers up after our writing session, just to make sure that no one will ever see them.

A friend of mine had a very difficult relationship with his father. His father was very cold and undemonstrative. My friend had longed to be close to his father all of his life and had suffered tremendous damage to his spirit as a result of not having this warm relationship. His father had never touched him as far back as he could remember. In fact, the only time he could remember being touched was during a beating. One day my friend was notified that his father had been rushed to the hospital with a severe and massive heart attack. While on the plane to his father's bedside he found a pad of paper in the seat pocket in front of him. Although the man had always scoffed at writing things down (this was stuff women did), while on the plane to the hospital, he wrote his father a letter describing all of the feelings he had about him, the longing for his companionship and closeness, and, then, put the letter in his suit pocket. When he arrived at the hospital, he made a note to himself that when he had an opportunity to talk to his father alone, he would share some of his feelings with him. The night of his arrival at the hospital, his father slipped into a coma and the next day he died. While sitting alone with his father in the mortuary, my friend stared at his father in the coffin, hating him as he had never hated him before. He remembered that he had the letter in his suit pocket. He walked over to the coffin and put the letter in the breast pocket of his father's jacket. When the family and close friends went to the grave site, he knew his letter would be buried with his father. While his father was being lowered into the ground, he remarked that it felt like thousands of pounds had been lifted from his shoulders.

With all of the demands and chaos of our own lives, many times our emotions become so jumbled, so chaotic, so puzzling, that the only way to flush out the confusion is to write all that jumble on paper. It is healthy, healing and can be a time of great creativity if we write it all down. There are lots of ways to do it:

- Write all the random words that come to mind.
- Write letters to people or yourself, but don't send them.
- Write in a journal to use as a kind of record of your life's journey.

It doesn't matter how you say it, or what you say, the most important thing is that you get it out of you and on to paper. If you never want anyone to see what you have said, tear it up and throw it away.

A woman shared with me her painful struggle with a divorce. She could not seem to rid herself of the anger and hatred she felt for her husband. So she sat down and wrote and wrote and wrote. After she had spent hours of venting on paper and felt finally resolved and cleansed, she tore the pages into little pieces, put them in a box and buried it in a big hole in her back yard. For her, that little ritual has given her enormous release and freedom from the hurt and anger that she experienced. It doesn't matter HOW you do it, just do it!

## SHARE FEELINGS APPROPRIATELY

The foundation of all relationships, effective or ineffective, is communication. And much of our stress comes from the lack of communicating our emotions and feelings appropriately. There are so many people who never really share their feelings, not because they don't want to but out of fear. They don't want to hurt other peoples' feelings. They fear conflict. They are afraid of losing the relationship. Or, they just may not know how to talk about feelings in an appropriate way. Couples won't talk about their emotional and physical needs. Children won't talk about disappointments with parents. Co-workers won't share expectations and disappointments. Employees won't confront bosses and vice versa. Friends won't share feelings or desires—all because we don't want to offend or alienate each other.

In learning how to share feelings appropriately, there are four elements to consider: 1) the event where something was said or done; 2) the feelings that were aroused as a result of what was said or done; 3) the behavior or words that occurred as a result of the feelings; and 4) the outcome of the behavior or words.

Whenever an event occurs, whether it is something that someone has said or done, it will give rise to either a positive or negative feeling. There is no way we can control that event or feeling. The next thing that happens is that it will trigger some kind of behavior on our part. Maybe the behavior is reactionary to the feeling in a negative way. Sometimes the behavior can be expressed by someone clamming up, or by someone becoming very explosive. Whatever the reaction, it will always have an outcome. What most people forget is that the behavior will have an outcome and the recipient of that behavior may never forget it.

Often in our lives we remember something that was said to us by a parent, grandparent, coach, teacher, or boss that may have been said casually or flippantly. That person may not remember what they said or did, but it can leave a mark on us that we will never forget. The same thing happens with us. We seem to forget that what we say or do may have an incredible impact on those who are the recipients. It is so important for us to stop and think about the outcome we are looking for in a relationship. In order to have more success in our communication, it is helpful to start with the outcome we want and work backward to the behavior required in order to ensure that outcome, rather than reacting first with the feelings and behavior.

A friend of mine, Janet, has beautiful strawberry blonde hair. Her daughter Chelsie also has her mother's beautiful hair. When Chelsie was a freshman in high school, she joined a particular peer group that gave her the sense of belonging that she needed. Desiring to belong, she came to the breakfast table one day with bright chartreuse colored hair. My friend, Janet, was stunned and angry. Many harsh words were said and both went away that morning very distraught. The situation did not get better because the cycle of events once begun continued, always giving rise to feelings and behavior that produced a negative outcome. One day Chelsie came home with bright fuchsia hair, another day black patent hair, but the final straw was when she shaved one-half of her hair off. At that point, Janet realized that she was not achieving the outcome for which she longed. She stopped and began to analyze more closely her reactions and how they were estranging her from her daughter.

She first realized that the issue was not so much that Chelsie was changing her hair, but that it was a direct negation of her (Janet's) hair. Janet perceived that Chelsie did not like having hair like her mother's, which felt to Janet like an attack on her self-esteem. The other realization was that whenever the two of them went out in public together, Janet was afraid that people would criticize her competency as a mother because of her "odd looking" daughter. Janet realized that the issue was really about her, not about Chelsie. And she also realized that she was losing one of the most important relationships in her life. She stopped and asked herself: "What is the outcome that I really want?" Her obvious answer was that she wanted the love and closeness with her daughter. With that realization, she made amends with her Chelsie.

The lesson here is to ask yourself: "What is the outcome that I really want?" And, "What kind of behavior will get me the outcome I'm looking for?"

### Say What You Think, Feel and Want

A handy model to follow in communicating feelings appropriately is as follows:

1. Acknowledge Intention—with most people in our lives, there is not a deliberate intention to hurt or be mean spirited. Therefore, it is most helpful if the statements in sharing feelings are, "I know it is not your intention to be rude, hurtful, unkind, or mean...."
2. Describe Behavior—"However, when you say or do (describe behavior)"
3. Describe Impact— "This is how it makes me feel or I perceive...."
4. Indicate Reaction—"I then react...."
5. What Will Change and Commitments Made?—"So, can we talk, make a commitment, have an agreement, resolve, etc?"

So, in Janet's situation, the conversation with Chelsie may have gone like this:

"Chelsie, I love you and care for you deeply. It is not my intention to hurt or embarrass you. I want to be close to you and understand you." (The truth about Janet's intention.)

"When you do these things to your hair," (Describe behavior) "It makes me believe that you hate your hair, and resent the fact that your hair is like mine. It makes me feel that you resent me for being the one that gave it to you." (Describe impact)

"So then I get defensive, hurt and angry because I don't believe you care about me. I'm not excusing my behavior, but describing my reaction." (Describe reaction)

"I realize that my love for you outweighs what you do to your hair, and I want to have our relationship back on track again. So just know that when you do that to your hair, it's not because I am trying to control you, it's about my feelings of hurt that you might not like what you inherited from me. I will not bother you any more about your hair. Our relationship is much more important to me." (What will change—what are commitments?)

Sometimes, we don't believe we have the right words to say, or that someone else is much better at expressing themselves than we are. But if we give ourselves some time to prepare for the conversation and practice the right words, we can't help but get better at it.

The most important factor to remember in sharing feelings or resolving conflict is to always remember to keep all parties' dignity and integrity intact. I realize this is not rocket science. It really boils down to treating people decently. However, sometimes in our zeal to be decent, we never get to the root of what is bothering us and it can eat away at us. Then when we least expect it, we lash out and say something harsh and cruel, or withdraw even more into ourselves until we make ourselves sick. The following suggestions are given to remind us to how to deal with our emotions appropriately:

### Clearly Identify Your Thoughts and Feelings

During the preparation of the interaction with the other party, it's helpful to make sure we are clear about what we want. There can be a tendency to whine or complain when we are not clear about what we want to have changed. Again, what do we want to see as an outcome or result of the conversation? What do we want to have happen?

## Ask, "What is the real motivation for me in this situation?"

It's very easy to do double-talk and avoid the real issues because we think we might be hurtful or we don't know what to say. If we use the model above to help us clarify and identify our thoughts we can more clearly state what we mean.

## Listen Carefully to the Other Person

Listening carefully and attentively to others is sometimes the hardest thing for me to do. I find myself looking at someone as if I'm really listening, but letting my thoughts about the person, his or her face, what feelings are being portrayed, clothing, (or whatever else) distract me so I'm not really paying attention to the words or meanings that person is conveying.

I also notice that so much of my energy goes into second guessing what someone really means. When I do this, I'm not really listening to the other person. I'm listening only to myself and projecting all of my own neediness into the conversation. Therefore, I really miss what the other person is trying to communicate to me.

## Choose Your Battles Carefully

A famous general once said, "Some hills are too small to die for." Many times the issue for us is being right and proving the other person wrong. Most of us carry signs around in each hand. The sign in one hand says "I'm right." The sign in the other hand says, "You're wrong." When I'm talking I put up my sign, "I'm right," and when you're talking I put up my sign "You're wrong." In order to create more effective communication, I must put down my signs. I must consider the outcome I am looking for. I ask myself if compromising the relationship is worth the battle.

I remember years ago when this fact first hit me. I was arguing with someone about a historical fact. I was hanging on to my "rightness" no matter what. As emotions rose, it occurred to me that the fact would be there with or without my arguing about it. Sooner or later the truth would be known and the important thing was to just let it go!

### Temporarily Shelve an Issue If Emotions Are Too High

In the above example, when I was arguing, it was clear that neither of us was listening because our emotions were too intense and overwhelming. Now, when I feel myself getting emotional, I move out of the way of the emotions, give myself some space to calm down, and approach the situation when we both are more in control, thoughtful and prepared.

### Avoid Dirty, Ineffective Tactics, or Compromising Behavior

There is a myth in Norway about trolls. Trolls are little creatures who create havoc for people by being mean and unkind. I have a little troll that comes out now and again when I am hurt or angry at someone. Actually, there's nothing wrong with having a troll, it's what I allow her to get away with that's harmful. I certainly don't want that troll to damage a valued relationship.

It is easy for people to play games and manipulate others. All of us know in our hearts what is ethical, or the right thing to do and what is wrong. For the sake of our own self-esteem, we must take the high road or the most ethical way.

### Remember the Value of "I" Statements

In any interaction with others, instead of using the attacking method of "you said, or you did, or it is your fault," try to use "I sense, I perceive, I believe, I think, I feel...." When we identify the concern or feelings as our own, and that the desire to resolve the problem is our desire, it is more apt to defuse defensiveness from the other person. The only way we can resolve issues effectively is not to get sucked into defensive reactions.

## Don't Tell Another Person What He/She Thinks or Feels, or "Should" Think or Feel

It is very easy when we are emotionally involved with those close to us, to give advice and dole out a good deal of "shoulds" and "oughts." I find it is so easy to tell people what they should or ought to do. However, when someone does it to me, even when I know they are right, I resist and get defensive. Why? Telling others what they should do is a very good way to bring out all of their defensive mechanisms and shut down listening. When I'm in the midst of pain and distress, I want someone to be empathic and caring. I am not interested in having them give me their advice. If I want advice, I'll ask for it.

So, even when you are convinced that you can be helpful, avoid words like "should" and "ought" and instead use phrases like, "Have you thought about...?" "What can I do to help you?"

## Avoid Triangulation

Triangulation means going to a third party to gain support for our side of the issue. Many times it means putting someone down to the third party in order to gain sympathy and an army of backers for our cause. This can be dirty tactics and is a good way to destroy the relationship as well as severely hurt the other person. If I have an issue with an individual, it is more ethical to direct my concerns to that person only and try to resolve my issues with them directly. If someone is using me as part of a conspiracy toward another, I ask that person to resolve it with that person with whom they are disagreeing instead of bringing me in to take sides.

In my consulting work with organizations, I hear story after story of how someone in a group has had his or her feelings hurt by a co-worker and then sets out to get others in the work group to censure that person by exclusion, biased perceptions and prejudices. Before long, the group is polarized, which causes major dysfunction on a team.

It takes time and a lot of practice to use these tools to share our feelings appropriately. But the more we practice, the more we will see very effective results in keeping everyone's dignity and integrity intact.

# Ask For Feedback

One of the hardest things to do is to ask for feedback from others, whether it is a boss, co-worker, lover, family member or friend. Asking others for their opinion about us can be very risky business so instead, we have a tendency to obsess and worry about what others think. This kind of worry and obsession is incredibly stressful. If I want to know what someone thinks about me, I need to ask. Sometimes I may just want to be affirmed. I may just want to know that someone loves or likes me. Whatever it is, start out with the reason for asking.

For example: "I don't want to make you uncomfortable, however, I'm wondering if you could give me some feedback about your perception of...(what you have said or some behavior).

"When I'm with you, I'm not sure how I come across, or how you perceive...behavior." "So, I'd like to know what you believe, see, perceive, or think about..." (what you say or do).

Sometimes, just a simple "Did what I say make any sense?" "Did what I say make you uncomfortable?" As with everything, practice helps.

# Manage Conflict Appropriately

Not only must we learn to share our feelings appropriately, but we also need to resolve the many types of conflict that confront us. There are interpersonal conflicts, internal conflicts, conflicts around making the right decisions, and conflicts of values, beliefs and attitudes. One of the quickest ways to get stressed is when we are in a conflict situation because, once again, we believe we are losing, or have lost, control or might make another person upset with us.

On the positive side, dealing with conflict in a productive way can make us feel good about ourselves and can push the envelope of change for us. It can certainly stimulate new levels of awareness and creativity. I have heard so many stories about people who have been in pain or conflict, and even though the process or transition of getting through it was hard, there most often seemed to be a positive ending. When I think about all of the very hard changes in my own life, I can remember times that I really did not believe I could survive. Then, when I was on the "other side" of the change, I discovered that I was much better off than I had been before. Of course, there are life events such as major physical challenges, death of loved ones or close friends that are not positive. But even very difficult transitions like finding a new job, developing new relationships or changes in life style can give us opportunities to be creative and find positive outcomes to what seems so overwhelming, stressful and hopeless at the time. The usual first thing that comes to our mind in the middle of these situations, however, is "What do I need to do to get away from it, or to fix it?"

I have already mentioned that stress originates in the way we think about things. It is helpful to ask ourselves, "What is the lesson here for me? What can I learn from this experience?" Believe me, I know it is not easy to be logical or sensible in the middle of the pain. Our brains seem to take our thinking off in every direction at once. The pain might be too overwhelming at the time, but at some point in the pain and hurt it works to look for the creative ways out of it, and what we might do to begin the solution process.

### Conflict Resolution Model

Because conflict can be so debilitating, I have found a model or process to follow in order to resolve the issue. I use it for everything in my life—whether it is in the professional work I do, or my personal life. This model helps me to find solutions.

This resolution model, also, is a helpful tool in any relationship to reach harmony and understanding. It is not only useful for intimate and close relationships, for internal work on issues that are difficult for you to resolve, but also for teamwork in any environment. Go through each of the steps asking clear questions at each point to clarify the issues so you can move toward some type of resolution. If conflict is not resolved, it will then start the cycle of hurt, confusion, negativity, cynicism, anger and hostility which is discussed on page 64.

Clarify/Vent

Assumptions vs. Reality/Facts

My Contribution

Desired Result

Explore Options

Make Commitments

Follow Through

*Step I: Clarify/vent/whine/complain/bellyache*

In order to get at what is bothering us, the first step is to "dump our stuff." It is important that the issues we are concerned about are put out on the table so it is easier to clarify. Sometimes we have feelings and reactions that we don't understand and until we get them out where we can get a better look at them, we can never get started in the resolution process. To clarify, vent and whine in a healthy and non-defensive way, use the model outlined on page 70. Another way to vent those feelings is to write them down, over and over until they become clearer.

When I work in organizations with dysfunctional or ineffective teams, it is important to allow each member of the team, or the team as a whole, to vent their concerns. This must be the first step. People cannot move forward and participate in any resolution process unless they have had a chance to be heard. We need to be acknowledged and reassured that our concerns are valid. Even if no one does anything about my concerns, specifically, it is important for me to know that someone heard them, acknowledged them and affirmed their validity.

### Step II: Assumptions vs. reality/facts

The next step is to clearly define the facts versus assumptions; the truth versus fiction; reality versus fantasy. Conflict can result due to a perception of an intention to hurt us. Because of our own internal needs, biases, values, etc., we might misread or misinterpret the intentions of others. Until we are clear about the facts, we cannot move forward to resolution. It is important to ask yourself or clarify with others, "What did the other person really say or do?" Before all parties move toward resolution of a situation, it is most critical to determine if there really is an issue at all. Sometimes we don't need to go any further because we realize we misunderstood the intentions.

### Step III: My contribution

Step #3 is the critical question of "What did I do to contribute to this problem?" Often the response is, "It's not my fault" or "I didn't do anything!" Right! Often we didn't do anything. We avoided the issue altogether. For all of us, it's important to examine the ways in which we may exacerbate a problem. Am I playing games, hiding the truth, not facing the truth about myself or just itching for a fight? What might I be doing that is contributing to the conflict or the lack of a resolution. And, then importantly, what can I contribute to the solution of the problem?

### Step IV: Desired result

The very important step in this process is to determine what it is we want to accomplish. What is it that we want to fix? What is the outcome we are looking for? What is the real issue we're trying to resolve? As mentioned earlier, it is critical that we are clear about what we want to accomplish in resolving this conflict. It's always easy to want to push to be right, but is that what I really want to accomplish? What's the real outcome I'm looking for?

*Step V: Explore options*

Once we have made it to this step, the rest is easy. When we begin to explore how we will get to the solution, or the outcome we both have agreed upon, it is necessary to explore ways of accomplishing it. What are the steps that need to be in place? Who will be responsible for what and how will it be accomplished? There are many ways to accomplish resolution. Brainstorming ideas and agreeing to compromise or collaborate, most of the time you can reach everyone's goals.

*Step VI: Critical first steps*

After discussing the options toward gaining a solution, a plan must be developed. The best way to begin to make a change is to look at the necessary first steps toward accomplishing the desired outcomes. So we look at the first steps that must be taken to move all parties forward. These need not be large steps, but doable ones to get the process started.

*Step VII: Make commitments and follow through*

The last and very important step in this process is for us to make commitments to each other. Make sure that all parties in this resolution process make the commitments that we have explored in Step V. It helps to set a time in the near future to check with each other to make sure we all feel good about the process and commitments that have been made. We then ask ourselves what's working? What's not working? What do we need to do differently?

## ANGER AS PART OF A DESTRUCTIVE LIFESTYLE

For many, the life of anger has become commonplace and addictive. Although some people may enjoy being negative and angry, for most of us, it is very stressful. As discussed in Chapter 3, anger is a terribly toxic substance that will eventually destroy us. I've been in a lot of work environments and I don't see that the behavior of ridiculing, carping, or making fun of people is accepted, in spite of what we see in the popular sitcoms.

It is easy to focus the cause of our anger on those outside of ourselves. There seems to be any number of things or people at which to be angry. We blame each other, the schools, doctors, lawyers, businesses, governments, everyone for what is wrong with the world today. We believe the causes for all of our misery rest with people or things outside of ourselves. The truth is, however, that when I am angry, it is about *me* and what is missing in *my* spirit. When you are angry, it's about *you* and what is missing in *your* spirit. Any time we are angry, the anger is coming from something triggered inside of us, not anyone else. There are times, of course, when anger is legitimate, but it is still being triggered from one or more of our needs. When the terrorists, for example, destroy people, you can bet I am angry! My safety needs are threatened. But it is still my anger.

Whenever someone else is angry, whether at you, or someone, or something else, it is not about you or me, it is about them. It is important that we remember we are not the cause of someone else's anger. We may just happen to be in the way at the time. This is not to imply that there are not times when people are justified in their anger. It is important to remember who is carrying the anger and realize that something has triggered one of their internal spirit needs. So get out of their way.

When I was growing up in Spokane, Washington the big event of the year was the annual snowball fight between the boys and the girls. Each year we found better ways to fortify our forts, make more lethal snowballs and practice our aim. The anticipation in the neighborhood always rose to a fevered pitch because everyone wanted to know who had used the latest technology in giving them the advantage over the other. When the snowball fight began, the girls invariably stood, hands on hips, defying the boys to throw the first snowball. And, of course, the boys always obliged. Instead of hiding behind our carefully crafted forts, we girls dared those snowballs to hit their targets. Of course, the snowballs always did. Do you think that we girls said to the boys, "Oh, that's okay, we forgive you"? Of course not! By being splatted with a snowball only meant that we now had an excuse to use our own "high-tech, lethal weapons." And then, the fight was on!

Communication is very much like a verbal snowball fight. We use our "high tech" verbal weapons to level our opponent. When someone is coming at you with their verbal snowballs...GET OUT OF THE WAY—DUCK!

### Defusing Anger

Since anger is directly related to stress, when we are angry and the emotion is overwhelming us, there are several techniques that will help us get past the emotion to guide us to a resolution.

### Disengage, Distract Yourself and Stop Negative Thoughts

Contrary to popular opinion, it is not healthy to blow up and "tell someone off." (For more information, read Redford Williams book, *Anger Kills,* referenced at the end of the chapter.) Talking with the individual or individuals to resolve the issue is important, but first one should calm down and move away from the emotion by getting away from the situation (or person) and removing themselves from the area. A common technique is to take a walk. While you're walking you can take deep breaths and try to think of something pleasant, sing a song either out loud or in your head—anything that will serve as a distraction. This distraction will only be temporary; but, before we can do anything definitively about the situation, we must calm down, and make ourselves think clearly.

### Get Away, Get Quiet and Write Things Down

Sometimes, when we are explosive, hurt, angry, or negative to any degree, it helps to get away and get quiet. I close my eyes, take deep breaths and say calming words to myself over and over or sing one of my theme songs. We can pick any word or any happy song that works for us. This helps to calm us down until we can begin to think about how to handle the situation. Another helpful tool is to write things down.

### Consider Facts and Reality, Not Assumptions

When I get really emotional about something, I find it helpful to stop and ask myself why I care so much. What are the facts and why am I reacting the way I am? Many times when we hear the whole story we realize that our perceptions may have been flawed. By listening carefully, we get a better perspective of the reality or the facts of a situation which creates better understanding.

### Find Your Sense of Humor

In the midst of pain and struggle against anger, it helps to find things that are either humorous or fun. Laughing defuses anger and is an important way to heal ourselves and relieve stress.

## Humor

When was the last time you really belly laughed? Much has been written about the importance of humor. Norman Cousins, famous for his work on the importance of humor, credited a sense of humor with healing his body when he was dying of a connective tissue disease. Research has found that laughter releases endorphins and creates a sense of well being and comfort. My friends, Russ and Carol Olin, have the ability to make people around them laugh much of the time. Whenever we are in their presence we know it will be a jolly time. Consequently, they both have numerous very close friends who thoroughly enjoy being with them. Russ is not a stand-up comedian…he just finds lightness in most things and is good natured and good humored.

In the every day intensity of keeping body and spirit together we need to find something that will bring good sound laughter to our spirit. One of the best ways to help ourselves smile or chuckle is to listen to little children laughing and giggling, buy a tape that always makes us laugh, try to be with people who laugh easily, or have an infectious laugh.

Humor is anything that makes us laugh, smile, or chuckle. It is what brings lightness, is fun, makes us feel safe, and brings enjoyment to us at the moment. Humor is not humor, however, when it is at someone else's expense or damages the character or well being of another. Healthy humor is fun and has the result of giving relief from tension. There are many ways to heal our spirit with laughter and fun.

### Do Things Out of the Ordinary

On a special day each month or each week, develop a special ritual such as breakfast at a special place. Once a week watch a video of an old TV program featuring Lucille Ball or the Three Stooges, or anything comical, over our lunch hour. Use a video camera and take pictures of people doing silly things around the house or work. Get their permission to show it later for everyone to see and enjoy. When things are tense in the workplace or at home, we can wear funny hats, wear costumes, do outrageous things with our clothes, hair or face. At home we can eat dinner on the floor by candlelight, use our best dishes with tablecloths, put names on all family members that are names of famous people and pretend that those people are at our home for dinner or coming to visit. We can fly kites, make funny paintings and drawings, and wear masks.

 THEME SONGS

A very handy tool to use when we begin to feel ourselves getting tense, anxious, angry and obsessive is to develop a little theme song. I know this may sound silly or too easy to some, but it really works. In order to find a theme song that is appropriate to you, think of your favorite song…it may be a gospel song, hymn, R&B, rap, pop, country, or classical. It is important that you find a phrase that fits you, that makes you feel good or happy.

Write that phrase down and paste it on your dashboard, your computer, your bathroom mirror, wherever you often have occasion to see it. Whenever you begin to feel those negative feelings, you can just start singing your little phrase over and over. Within seconds, you will begin to feel better and stop the obsessing and nobody ever needs to know you're having a little party in your head!

## WALLOWING

Long ago, several close friends and I packed enough food and drink to last two weeks while running rapids in rafts on the Colorado River in the Grand Canyon. The trip was exhilarating...so exhilarating in fact, that when we got back to Colorado we all decided that we could do the Colorado River in the Grand Canyon in kayaks. In order to handle a kayak one must wear a helmet and life jacket and be skilled at right-siding the boat if it tips in a rapid. This technique is called rolling. In spite of the instructor's tenacity while teaching us in the pool to learn to roll, I never learned how. Our group decided that if we were to become truly proficient at this kayaking business, we needed three Olympic champion kayakers to teach us at a kayak camp. We went to the King's River outside of Fresno, California, for four days and three nights. We eagerly arrived, ripped our boats off of the vans, threw on our helmets and jackets and with oars in hand, trudged off to make our first run down the river. While I was walking to our embarking point, I looked at the river and decided that this surely was the time I would die. It looked like Niagara Falls to me! While I was surveying the river, the instructor walking next to me must have felt the terror coming from me because he said, "Are you scared?" "No, I said, I'm terrified!" He told me that if and when I should "dump" in the river and find myself in a "suck hole," that I should swim to the bottom of the river and go forward. (I thought to myself that if I were already drowning, I'd get to the bottom soon enough without swimming there intentionally.)

When we arrived at our embarking point, I was the last one to get into my boat and started to paddle out. Within seconds, I hit a deep hole, lost control of my boat and capsized. Since I did not know how to roll, I pushed myself out of the boat and found myself in the middle of a suck hole unable to get out. In the midst of my panic, I remembered what the instructor had said to me and miraculously, went to the bottom of the river and swam forward. A most amazing thing happened! First of all the bottom of the river was perfectly quiet. If you have ever been near rapids, you know that even when someone's mouth is in your ear, it is very difficult to hear them. Secondly, it was very still. I skimmed along the bottom, came up the other side of the rapid and continued bobbing down the river. What a great lesson that taught me!

1. Whether I am in the deepest despair or just having a bad day, I'll find the greatest sense of peace and serenity when I just dive deep inside myself and let go.
2. When I am in a bad mood, feeling sorry for myself, or feeling depressed, I just go to the bottom of the feeling and allow myself to wallow.

Wallowing is important because it allows us to let go of those things we are obsessing about. If we keep fighting whatever it is that is bothering us by trying to keep a "stiff upper lip" or defend against any of the emotions we might be experiencing, it only serves to stuff it and the pain has no expression or way out. Paradoxically, one way to relieve the obsession is to obsess about it until we finally get sick of it or wallow in it until we can finally let go of it.

It is important that we wallow appropriately. If we are going to take the time to feel sorry for ourselves, we need to make sure we have the necessary props. What is the most sure-fire way to make us feel really pitiful? Is it an old favorite movie that makes us cry? Is it a book, or some memory? How about all those songs that make us cry and feel sorry for ourselves? Then we need to put on our rattiest clothes—that old sweatsuit with the coffee stains and holes, the old bathrobe with grape jelly on it,

and get into the sob scene. Really go for it! Remember all the bad things that have ever happened to us, tell ourselves how awful everything is. We keep doing this until finally, we just get sick of it. Sometimes it is helpful during this wallowing time to write letters to ourselves telling ourselves how pathetic we are and how the whole world has done us wrong. After we have wallowed, it is sometimes helpful to take a nap, take a shower, take a walk, or do whatever we need to do to get active again. Some people have been known to take several minutes a day to wallow before they are able to move out of the dark spell in their lives.

If we are very fortunate, we can wallow with a close friend or loved one which can be very therapeutic. It must be someone we can trust, who will be sympathetic, and allow us to become disgusting in our self pity. Eventually we will get to the point where we are sick of ourselves and will want to move on. An added advantage is that our friend may give us a clue when it's time to stop the wallowing.

Wallowing is important to help us to not ignore the feelings of sadness and despair that often overwhelm us. For those of us who battle with depression, sadness, or just a case of the blahs from time to time, wallowing is a technique to consciously help us to get to the most inner part of ourselves, the inner spirit.

## WHAT'S THE WORST THING THAT CAN HAPPEN?

Finally, many times when I'm in the midst of a string of things that are especially stressful, I think of what is the worst thing that can happen to me? If my family is okay, my health is okay, my friends are okay, then I can make it through one more day. I say to myself, "Well, at least it's not...(whatever the worst thing could be)."

# When Nothing Helps

For some, the depression, sadness, despair is beyond just being able to wallow about it for a short period of time. If you find that the depression is overwhelming and lasts for long periods of time, I urge you to consult your physician. There is help for you! The chemistry in the brain is fickle and unpredictable. Because of prolonged stress, the chemistry of our brains can become unbalanced. In that situation, please consult your doctor who will be able to help you through the crisis with medications that can stabilize your emotions and give you a chance to gain control of your life.

*References:* Brinkman, Rick, Kirschner, Rick. *Dealing With People You Can't Stand.* Just as the title suggests, the authors give good suggestions in how to deal with difficult people.

Bolton, Robert. *People Skills.* This book is a classic on interpersonal relationships. A must for everyone's library.

Fisher, Roger, Brown, Scott. *Getting Together.* Although this book is about negotiating, it has wonderful suggestions for all interpersonal interactions.

Bramson, Robert M. *Coping with Difficult People.* Another good book on the subject.

Bloomfield, Harold with Leonard Felder. *Making Peace with Your Parents.* The title is misleading because this book has many good insights into why we carry around resentments and anger toward others—especially those with whom we are close.

Augsberger, Davide. *When Caring is Not Enough: Resolving Conflicts Through Fair Fighting.* Gives great suggestions in how to resolve conflicts with people close to you.

Lerner, Harriet Goldhor. *The Dance of Intimacy.* Wonderful advice on how to manage intimate relationships.

La Roche, Loretta. *Life is Not a Stress Rehearsal.* If you have ever heard Loretta speak you know how funny she can be. Her books give wonderful suggestions in how to find fun and humor in everyday living.

La Roche, Loretta. *Relax: You May Only Have a Few Minutes Left.*

Simon, Sidney B. *Getting Unstuck: Breaking Through Your Barriers to Change.* Good insight on how to manage change.

Williams, Redford, Williams, Virginia. *Anger Kills.* An excellent book describing how anger breaks down one's immune system and destroys physically.

# 6   HEALING THE SPIRIT
## Stress Reducers for the Spirit

*The problem is how to remain whole in the midst of the
distractions of life; how to remain balanced,
no matter what centrifugal forces tend to pull one off center;
how to remain strong, no matter what shocks
come in at the periphery and
tend to crack the hub of the wheel.*
Anne Morrow Lindbergh

The most basic, fundamental part of us is our Spirit. It is the
Me, the Self. It houses our personality, our values, beliefs and
attitudes and the basic needs of positive self-esteem, a sense
of security, a belief we are competent, ability to trust, and love.
It sets the tone of who we are and how we approach things. It
is the foundation of our Self that motivates our thinking and
behavior. Whenever we are stressed, it will always relate back to
our perception of how our fundamental five Spirit needs are or
are not being met. Thinking about the fulfillment of our Spirit
needs is not something that can be clearly or easily defined and
understood. Hopefully, the following explanation will help you
see how your own behavior is related to the fulfillment or lack of
fulfillment of one or more of your Spirit needs.

In considering all of our Spirit needs, it is rare that all of them
are met at one time. As I mentioned in the last chapter, when I
am angry it is about me. If someone else is angry and I just happen to be in the way, it is not about me it is about the other person. Whatever negative behavior is exhibited, it all goes back to
the fact that one or more of my, or the other person's, Spirit needs
are not being met. So how does one heal the pain when one or
more of the Spirit needs are missing?

This process of healing our internal Spirit is not easy. Why are
self-help books so popular? Because we are all looking for THE
ANSWER. I know I am! Part of the answer comes from our

understanding of what's going on inside of us—under the surface of the iceberg. If you remember the analogy of the iceberg on pages 16 and 20, you will remember that the Spirit needs are in the subconscious. That means that we are not conscious of them. They operate continually within us, but we are not paying attention to them at the conscious level. However, we can bring them to our consciousness by thinking about them when our attention is drawn to them.

## DEVELOPING POSITIVE SELF-ESTEEM

Even though positive self-esteem doesn't cure stress, it most certainly will help to manage it. Developing self-esteem is both simple and difficult! Any self-help book will have something about how to understand or fix self-esteem. I have discovered that it really boils down to these simple, but hard-to-do truths:

### Facing Our Fears and Trolls

The most destructive element to positive self-esteem is fear. These fears will sabotage our sense of positive well-being and cripple us in successful living. We may think that we can get rid of them by burying or ignoring them, but just because we bury fears, doesn't mean they are dead. It's time to weed them out! There are so many fears that plague us—fear of failure, fear of what people think, fear of consequences for past objectionable behaviors, fear of what might happen, fear of rejection—all of these fears begin to become our obsessions.

I'm afraid of being financially destitute, or as I mentioned earlier, that people will reject me. Even though I know where it comes from, it doesn't help when my little trolls take advantage of those fears and try to convince me they are true. The minute those little trolls start their song and dance, I take time to write my fears down on paper. Then I talk to myself and remind myself of what is real. I also find that talking to a friend or my family helps. In the writing and talking about it, I learn to objectify it and see the fear for what it really is—a fear, not a reality.

I certainly do not intend to minimize the power of fear in our lives. I have mentioned many times that fear is a root cause of stress. But, once again, it's how I view the situation, how I think about the situation that creates the reality for me. So, it is important that I do everything I can to objectify the issue so I can begin to develop ways to manage the situation. That's why talking and writing about it can be so helpful.

### Making Amends and Reconciliation

The second way to build self-esteem is to say "I'm sorry" when appropriate. How many times have we asked for forgiveness for something we did or said and really meant it? Remember how liberating and cleansing it felt? Being genuinely sorry for words and behavior and expressing it, releases enormous amounts of negative energy that get in the way of developing our positive self-esteem. A tremendous amount of negative energy, which saps our self-esteem, goes into carrying guilt, shame and resentfulness.

In my assessment and analytical work in organizations, when it is clear that managers, executives, or employees have said or done things that have been hurtful, these folks find it almost impossible to say they have been wrong or hurtful and apologize. Others in the organizations would more easily be able to move on, to be productive, to be energized, if only the offending person was able to simply say "I'm sorry."

Without the act of repentance, there can be no process of forgiveness thereby enabling all parties to move forward. To heal self-esteem, we must cleanse ourselves of hurts caused to others and to ourselves.

The reconciliation process may be painful. It is painful to ask for forgiveness and, sometimes, it is painful to give it to both ourselves and others. In these situations, it might, at the very least, be helpful to write a letter to that person asking for forgiveness, but not send it. Truly allowing ourselves to feel the hurt that we may have caused others or ourselves, is in itself a beginning of the healing process to our self-esteem.

## Knowing/Defining Our Purpose

Each one of us has special gifts and abilities that can contribute to the growth of others and can positively impact the world we live in. We may never find ourselves on the cover of the daily newspaper, but each day that we give of our particular gifts, we are contributing to the forward movement of goodness and wholeness to those around us. We may believe that we have nothing particularly special to contribute. However, some of the most powerful and effective leaders in the world did not think of themselves as particularly special. Mahatma Gandhi was a mediocre lawyer in South Africa when he had a powerful experience that awakened him to the suffering of people, particularly his own people of India.

Rosa Parks was an African American domestic who traveled by bus every day to go to work in a white neighborhood in Montgomery, Alabama. One day she refused to sit at the back of the bus as she was required, and that act catapulted the Civil Rights Movement into the consciousness of the American people.

A young woman in the hills of Kentucky with three children heard a news broadcast about the people in Russia who were unable to buy food and fuel because they were so poor. She was so moved by the story that she decided to find a way to send someone in Russia a box of chocolates and coffee. At first everyone thought she was crazy to try to send a small box of food to one individual in Russia. Through her tenacity and will, three years later thousands of American and Russian families are paired up giving and receiving food, clothing and books.

Once there was a man who was very skilled at making doll cradles. Many people offered to pay him a handsome sum of money for his cradles. He refused however, and would only give his cradles to little girls in residential treatment centers for the mentally and emotionally challenged. This was his gift and it gave both him and the little girls great pleasure. Another woman who believed she had no gifts made wonderful brownies that people encouraged her to sell. She refused however and only made her brownies for the Girl Scout troops in her area. A family of men in their sixties and seventies who, when young, used to sing together in church, now go to rest homes to sing for the residents.

These people may not be considered gifted. They are not the world's intellectuals, nor are they among the rich and powerful. They are ordinary people like you and me who saw a need and did something to contribute. All of us have a gift—whether we can make something, write something, or hold someone—we must find what our special talent is and use it. It is the sharing of these gifts that brings healing, first to us, then to others.

Because there are so many ways we can make a contribution, it is sometimes hard to find a place where our particular skills might be most useful. What things give us the greatest delight and joy? It may be cooking, working with crafts, building things, writing poetry, singing, telling stories, playing a musical instrument. We may have a special yearning to work with a certain group of people, the elderly, children, babies, or people in need.

A friend of mine was a little league coach for a team of disadvantaged young boys. One summer, while he was their coach, the team won the state championship. He recounts the memory that when he was standing on the field holding the trophy high in the air with all the little kids and their parents and friends swarming around him, it was one of the most exhilarating and emotional moments of his life. He knew that he had made a difference in their lives and the hard work and discipline with those little boys had paid off. He put the trophy away and over the years forgot about that very significant time when he knew he had made a difference. One day as he rummaged through some old boxes, he found the trophy. He put that trophy on his desk at work to remind him of that very special time. He made the commitment to go back to his coaching again, and once again, he has found a sense of serenity and joy in his life.

Giving of our gifts is a way of loving others which creates a sense of goodness in ourselves, thereby strengthening our self-esteem.

### Increasing Self-Discipline

I like being a slug and lying around doing nothing. However, I feel better about myself when I get things done and keep my commitments, not only to myself, but also to others. Discipline is about sticking to commitments and promises. When we promise to do something with or for our children, spouse, friend, boss, or co-worker, and we follow through, it makes us feel good about ourselves. This is building our self-esteem. When we break commitments or promises, we compromise a value that in the end takes a nick out of our self-esteem. So how many promises have we kept lately? How many commitments have we kept? Notice how it helps to keep stress levels down and makes us feel good about ourselves!

### Being Authentic

Authenticity is being open and honest concerning who we really are. My daughter, Heidi, has never known how to lie, misrepresent herself, or withhold what she sees as major inconsistencies or duplicity in herself or others. In our family and with friends she has truly raised the bar in interpersonal relationships. She absolutely cannot ignore an issue when she believes that something is not right. When most everyone I know, including myself, will overlook things that are uncomfortable or may be confrontational, she will not. The outcome of her commitment to total openness and honesty is that everyone wants to be her friend and knows that they can absolutely trust her. The lesson for me is that relationships are cleaner, and our own self-esteem is stronger when we know that we are being truly who we are. If we are not consistent, honest and ethical about who we are, we lose something valuable to our self-esteem. This does not negate, however, what I said in the last chapter about not exploding in anger even when you believe it is justified. We can still be authentic by expressing our anger appropriately thereby keeping everyone's dignity and integrity intact.

Sometimes people use the banner of honesty to be cruel or mean spirited. That is not being authentic. When people say or do cruel things to others, it is coming from some unmet need within. As discussed in the last chapter, it is really about them not the recipient of their cruelty.

Being authentic also means we are committed to live in an ethical way; doing what we know to be the right thing to do. I notice that when I do the right thing, I feel so much better about myself and I don't have to worry about what I did or said. I believe that deep in the heart of most of us is the knowledge of what is the right thing to do and when we behave according to that standard, we build strong self-esteem.

### Being Courageous

Not many of us will ever appear on the cover of the newspaper expounding our heroic deeds. But every day we have the opportunity to display acts of courage. And every day most of us perform small acts of courage. Every time we exhibit courage in the little acts of our daily lives, we add another brick to our self-esteem. Whenever we leave our children at the daycare center in order to support our family when we really want to spend more time with them, we are courageous. Getting up every morning and going to work to give our best, displays courage. Telling the insensitive jokester that the comments made about a person or persons is not acceptable to us is displaying courage. Standing up for our beliefs is being courageous; and, many people are manifesting that kind of courage every day. That kind of courage builds self-esteem.

Self-esteem doesn't develop all at once. It takes persistence—plugging away at it day after day. Developing positive self-esteem is a process. And it is knowing that we are developing positive self-esteem that builds a strong foundation in handling stress in our lives.

## CREATING SECURITY

Everyone is talking about security. Remember, that the causes of stress are believing we are out of control and that we are overwhelmed. When we believe we are not safe, whether it is financially, physically, mentally or emotionally, we feel we have lost control of our own destiny and it can cause us stress. Having a sense of security is absolutely critical to the well-being of the spirit.

## $¢ Developing Financial Security

In today's times of job insecurity, people are struggling more and more with the fear of not having enough to live on throughout their lives. The media is full of doom about the demise of social security, the national debt, and other financial woes that affect us. Futurists tell us that by the year 2030 our life expectancy will be 130 years old! It is important that we believe that we can take care of ourselves. Statistics tell us that without a paycheck, many of us are two months away from being homeless.

There are many books and resources available to start a savings program no matter how old we are. If we need help with financial matters, we better begin now. Knowing that we have begun a program and are putting something away every month will give us a sense of financial security. Once we get started, we may be motivated to save more over time.

## Maintaining Physical Security

There are lots of ways that people feel physically insecure. Sometimes we feel unsafe in the neighborhood where we work. Sometimes we feel afraid in our cars and homes. If we are in a place where we feel physically threatened, we must make immediate plans to protect ourselves by removal from the situation or by security devices to help us feel safer. These security devices can be cars with alarms, carrying a cellular phone at all times, special security locks on doors and windows and living in buildings with a good security system. If we can afford it, we need cars that are in good working condition to lessen the possibility of a breakdown.

If our physical security is being threatened by a spouse, lover, parent, or anyone else, we must take immediate steps to get away from the abuser and call the national Domestic Violence Hotline (1-800-799-SAFE). For the sake of the essence of who we are, we need immediate help! People who are abusers will not stop until they get help, and we are not the one who can help them!

### Understanding Emotional/Mental Security

Emotional and mental security are harder to understand and grasp. I have talked with hundreds of employees from many different organizations and am amazed that so many have said that it is not the company or their bosses that stress them or cause anxiety. Many dread going to work every day because they are not accepted by their peers, or they are not on the "in" crowd and go home from work feeling emotionally and mentally abused or just plain lonely. This can make going to work very stressful.

It is important that if we are feeling emotionally and mentally unsafe in an environment that we develop mechanisms to manage it. First, ask why am I feeling emotionally and mentally insecure? What are the actual events or words that cause me to be insecure? What or who has power over me? Why have I given that person, persons or entity the power over me? Is the perception real? If so, what can I do about it? What steps do I need to begin in order to feel safe? What do I need to do to get the power back? One way to develop the confidence we need to take steps to create security for ourselves is to learn to be competent.

## DEVELOPING COMPETENCE

Believing we are competent is a fundamental aspect of our spirit that needs constant vigilance. With everything moving so fast in our world, it is very clear that it is difficult to keep up with new techniques and knowledge that will contribute to the skills and abilities that we need to survive. And the fear that we may not be competent causes stress. This need for survival is not just in the realm of work. It is important to believe that we are competent as a parent, lover, spouse, daughter or son, friend, student, or whatever role we perform. When we believe or perceive that we may not be competent in any of the areas of our lives, it begins a cycle that impacts all other areas of our spirit. For example, if we believe that we are not as knowledgeable as we ought to be on the job, it can cause us to feel insecure, which in turn can affect our self-esteem. Therefore, it is important that we do all that is possible to keep ourselves competent in the areas that are important to us.

There are many institutions that offer courses, training and education in just about any area we might need. Local recreational centers, county agencies, schools and universities offer courses in parenting, how to study, computer technology, vocational skills, and many other areas to help us learn better skills. Many organizations provide training programs for a variety of skills to help people become better trained in their areas of expertise. If we take advantage of all the training we can get, we can have a better sense of being in control of our lives. It doesn't mean that we will know everything we need to know for our job or the other roles we may perform, but it certainly will add to our knowledge and our sense of self-esteem, which of course, reduces stress!

## DEVELOPING TRUST

Another important spirit need is the need to trust and be trusted. To be in community with others that one can trust is incredibly healing to the spirit. This community can be a work team, a family, or a group of friends. And, when we trust someone it certainly relieves stress. Once again, however, developing and keeping trust demands nurturing and diligence from those involved.

The dictionary describes trust as: *confidence, faith, to rely or depend upon.*

We know that trust is the foundation of any healthy relationship and when it is missing the relationship suffers. I believe that one of the most important reasons someone is admired, respected and sought after is because they can be trusted. My dear friends,

Russ and Carol Olin, continually astound me with their vast circle of incredibly interesting and admirable friends. Over the years of knowing and watching them I find that part of their secret is that they are absolutely trustworthy as well as ethical and honest. They know how to keep confidences. I know they are that way with everyone they know and consequently enjoy great and meaningful friendships.

So what does it mean to be trustworthy? It means being ethical, bone honest and authentic about ourselves and to be absolutely diligent to keep confidences that people share with us. If anyone suspects that we do not hold information and conversations absolutely confidential, we can be sure they will not trust us completely.

Although admirable, it is not enough to be trustworthy. Someone may be ethical, honest and authentic and I still will not trust them because I may not be sure that I can trust them with who I am. If I share my innermost thoughts with someone will they laugh at me, think I'm stupid, or secretly or openly criticize and judge me? If I cannot trust another with my whole self, I will hold back and distance myself from him/her. I find this so common in marriages and other relationships. Couples begin to drift apart because one of the members does not trust the other with his/her thoughts and feelings.

A true sense of wholeness is hard to accomplish without having at least one trusting relationship with someone. Part of being affirmed in one's being is knowing that there is at least one person we can trust fully to support and care for us, and with whom we can be open, honest, and respectful, and they with us. If we do not have anyone who fits this description, it is important to cultivate a relationship with someone who will. Most often this person is a best friend, or family member. But sometimes a trusting relationship can be formed with a pastor, therapist, teacher or co-worker. The important issue, however, is that we have someone in our lives whom we trust.

## LOVING OTHERS

The greatest power in the world is the power of love and loving. For true nurturing of the spirit, it is important to love and be loved. Love is a need not a want. It is not a "nice to have" or "I'll pick some up someday." Humankind cannot live well and wholly without some kind of loving. Loving deeply and intensely can be with a child, partner, a family member, a friend, or even with God. A good way to start the loving relationship is through spending time with that person and saying to that person often, "I love/like you." Love and well being are inextricably combined. The act of loving releases positive chemicals in the body to give one the sense of well being and goodness. It is very difficult, if not impossible, to hate while loving at the same time.

The interesting dichotomy is that when one is truly loving another, rather than being vulnerable, as so many would believe, one is truly the most powerful. You probably know, or know of, many people who have truly unconditionally and unselfishly loved another. In knowing these people, we find that it was their loving that made them powerful and strong to us, not weak. When I have been the most stressed, being with my girls has helped the most. There were times when I thought I couldn't go on but just knowing I had them, knowing they loved me and I loved them, kept me going.

I have met people over the years who believe there is no one in their lives to give love to, and that no one loves them. If this sounds like you, it might be helpful to find a place to volunteer that appeals to you, or get an animal to love. One woman I remember, particularly, told me she had no family and no friends. Her only life was her job. One day she woke up realizing that her life was empty and lonely. She decided to get a dog from a near-by animal shelter. Over a period of time, the shelter would call her about other dogs who needed a home so she became their ambassador to find suitable homes for dogs. Suddenly, for her, her life became meaningful. Her animals needed and loved her, she loved them, and the shelter had a volunteer who cared deeply for the dogs.

Millions of words have been written about the power of love, and what people of all ages will do and sacrifice in order to get it. There's no way I could ever do justice to this subject. One thing I do know is all of us want and need to be loved and to love, and the simplest way to be loved is to give it. This does not mean that we give objects to show love to others, it is essentially about affirming the being of another. There are many ways that we can affirm the being of another:

### Understand Their Stories

I have found that many people today are so self-absorbed that they cannot understand the meaning of empathy or do not have the ability to see the world from another's perspective. When we are self-absorbed, we tend to view other peoples' behavior as an attack or a response or reaction on us personally, when perhaps their behavior is a result of some pain or problem they might be perceiving or experiencing internally.

Longfellow said "If we could read the secret history of our enemies, we should find in each man's life sorrow and suffering enough to disarm all hostility." Everyone comes from a degree of suffering, pain and sorrow that may have caused their behavior to be the way it is. It does not mean that we need to accept negative or destructive behavior, but it helps to know the story and history behind the individual that caused that behavior in the first place. By understanding their stories, it helps to relate, understand and have kinship with others.

### Appreciate Their Uniqueness

Have we told that special person why they are special? What are the ways that make them special to us? List their gifts and talents. Describe what they do and can do that makes them unique and able to make a special contribution to this life. One of my clients manages a large group of employees. Before she became their manager her employees had been mentally and emotionally abused by another manager. She turned the department around, in part, by simply telling these employees how great and valuable they were.

### Listen to Them without Editorializing

 Sue Atchley Ebaugh said, "The greatest gift we can give one another is rapt attention to one another's existence." This "rapt attention" is not just staring into another's face and taking on the behaviors that might give the illusion we are listening to them in a patronizing way. Rapt attention is listening from the bottom of our being to the bottom of their being. In listening to the words, pay attention to the facial expressions, the tone of voice, the meanings behind the words, and especially the experiences and history from whence the words come.

It's important to understand that many times when we want to give an opinion, or change a person's mind, it is for our affirmation not theirs. To truly listen to another, we must set ourselves aside in the process. This does not mean that we become a stump and have no interaction. We are talking about showing others we love them by listening to them and engaging in dialogue that affirms their being, whether we agree with their ideas and beliefs or not. It is very difficult, if not impossible, to pay attention to another when we are absorbed in ourselves.

I'm not saying this is easy because we want so much to give advice and opinions. I have to stop and remind myself that people don't need my wisdom or opinions, they need my support and affirmation. The best ways to get started is to say "I love you," "I like you," "I care about you," and really mean it. Loving is a powerful way to heal our spirit and relieve stress.

I have given you an in-depth description of the five spirit needs. In reviewing them, you may believe that your self-esteem is strong, therefore the idea or concept of spirit needs does not apply to you. Or you may be in a loving relationship with your family and so you dismiss the idea that your negative behavior at work today is related to missing spirit needs because you have good self-esteem and loving relationships. The negative behavior you exhibited might be related instead to the fact that you perceived that someone does not think you are competent in a particular area, or that you feel intimidated by a person or group of persons at work, therefore feel insecure. Whatever behavior you exhibit at any time, whether positive or negative, is related to one or more of your spirit needs.

**References:** These are many books on self-esteem. The following are just a few:

McGraw, Phillip C. *Self Matters: Creating Your Life from the Inside Out.*

Schiraldi, Glenn R., et al. *The Self-Esteem Workbook.*

Branden, Nathaniel. *Six Pillars of Self-Esteem.*

Sorensen, Marilyn J. *Breaking the Chain of Low Self-Esteem.*

Dyer, Wayne. Anything by Wayne Dyer will be helpful to you.

Chopra, Deepak. Deepak has written many books. Check out the ones that look the most interesting to you.

# HEALING THE MIND
## Stress Reducers for the Mind

*If ignorance is bliss, why aren't there more happy people?*
Milton Berle

## CHECKLIST

In front of each statement, put one of three initials: E = I'm doing excellently in this; OK = I'm doing acceptably, but there's room for improvement; NS = This is an area where I definitely need strengthening.

_____ I enjoy a sense of wonder, a childlike curiosity that makes learning new ideas and skills energizing.

_____ I regularly exercise my artistic, playful and creative muscles by playing an instrument, singing, designing, writing, building, sewing, repairing broken items, or any activity that is creative.

_____ I enjoy using my mind to "spark off" new ideas with others by spirited dialogue and debate with stimulating people.

_____ I regularly balance my rational, analytical, verbal, quantitative left-brain functioning with intuitive, playful, non-analytical right-brain activities, such as music, drawing, gardening, joking, storytelling, imaging.

_____ I check out my perceptions of events and people with those I trust, to increase the likelihood that my understanding is based on the real situation I face.

_____ I enjoy stretching my mental and intellectual horizons by reading, thinking, and wrestling about tough issues outside of my everyday experience.

### Using Your Findings

Scan the three types of initials to get an overall feel for your mental self-care and fitness. Give yourself a mental pat on the back for the E items. Go through the OK and NS items, picking out those which seem important to you, jotting these down to generate ideas concerning what you might do to strengthen your creativity in those areas. (Howard Clinebell, Ph.D, *Well Being*)

When I speak of the mind, I'm referring to the intellectual part of you, the part that thinks, rationalizes, intellectualizes and objectifies. The mind interprets meaning in all of the events in our lives. Sometimes the mind is a fickle partner because it may perceive that something is stressful to us, when perhaps to others, the event is not stressful at all, as I discussed in Chapter 1 in using the roller coaster example. And, it is those interpretations that can cause us stress. The mind plays a very powerful role in how we manage stress, so it is necessary that we keep it active and healthy.

For many years it was believed that human brain cells began to atrophy at the age of 55. Now, however, researchers are finding that not only are we expected to live longer (perhaps until 130 years old), but our brain cells do not necessarily atrophy provided they are continually stimulated. So, how do we keep our mind stimulated, strong and healthy? We exercise it by learning new skills.

Richard M. Restak, M.D. in his book *The Mind* states, "At birth the human brain contains perhaps as many as one hundred billion nerve cells (some believe the figure to be fifteen billion). From then on there is a continuous process of attrition. Brain weight decreases gradually but surely—about 10% over a normal lifespan —because of neuron death. But not every part of the brain loses neurons at the same rate. In most brainstem regions—areas located below the cerebral cortex that are responsible for automatic unlearned activity—there is little or no cell loss with advancing age. The cerebral cortex, including the motor cortex and the frontal lobes (the thinking part of the brain), loses neurons at a maximum rate of fifty thousand a day." This may seem scary when you multiply this by 80 years, but scientists have found that the brain has a remarkable way of sustaining memory and thinking skills if it is exercised. We can hold off the aging process of the brain if we continually give it new experiences or learn new things.

We all know older people who remain active in some aspect of their work, find a continuing sense of purpose and are motivated to depend upon themselves and their own resources to stay vibrant and alert longer. It is also important to maintain a strong involvement with family and friends, flexible attitudes and an active rather than a passive life style (walking or exercise routines, a weekly bridge game rather than mindless hours staring at television ). These are key factors in maintaining mental sharpness. Put another way, "Use it or lose it." That's the bottom line of a twenty-eight-year study of four thousand people on Puget Sound in the state of Washington carried out by Professor K. Warner Schaie, of Pennsylvania State University (cited in *The Mind*, Richard M. Restak, M.D.).

Schaie found social involvement played a major part in maintaining mental vigor. Elderly people who live with their families or maintain an active social life outperformed their contemporaries who lived alone. The greatest decline was among widowed housewives who had never had a career of their own and led restrictive, often reclusive lives. Schaie believes that mental exercises, like

physical exercises, can help older people sustain and in some instances even improve their mental capabilities. This belief has been recently substantiated in the February, 2004 issue of *Popular Science*. Scientists have found that brain fitness depends on physical exercise, competitive sports, aerobics and other physical activities.

Mental deterioration comes from isolation, boredom and lack of intellectual challenge. People who still find wonder in life, have interests and are curious have a much greater chance of having a vibrant and active mind. A group of nuns living in an abbey in Minnesota typically live into their 90's and some even into the  100's enjoying very active and healthy memories and aptitude. The common thread for the mental health came from a continual exercising of the mind through solving puzzles together, practicing their memory skills, challenging each other in thinking tasks and being in a supportive, caring environment.

## Be a Perpetual Student

When I was a little girl I told my mother I couldn't wait until I was 40 years old. I believed that by then I would know everything I had to know and wouldn't have to study any more. Most everyone hates being a beginner. We look forward to the time when we can master a topic or skill. However, scientists tell us

that it is the very act of being a beginner, i.e. learning that keeps our mind active and our brain cells firing.

To keep the mind healthy, always have something that you are learning or planning to learn—whether it is a new skill or studying a new subject. There are many ways to learn new things while having fun doing them. Learn a new sport or language. Stretch your platform of knowledge. Find something you've never done before and become an expert in that field.

# REMEMBERING

My friends and I joke with each other that our memory is fading...that we are having a "senior moment." Although I might poke fun at myself, deep down there really is a fear that I will lose more and more of my ability to remember even the most basic things—such as my children's names! There are some things that we can do to stack the deck in our favor when it comes to remembering.

1. *Pay attention.* When I am meeting someone for the first time and get distracted by people in my peripheral vision, or with chatter in my own head, it is impossible for me to remember the person's name, let alone what they said. So, it helps to have some tricks to help us stay focused on that person. Whenever you can, repeat the person's name. If you can, introduce her to someone else. If you forget her name while talking to her, just ask her to tell you her name again. I have never known anyone to be offended if you ask them to repeat their name again to you.

2. *Associate.* Whenever we try to remember someone's name or facts, or any other data, it sometimes is helpful to associate the information with something we already know and are familiar with. For example, when I'm remembering a list of things, I take the first letter of each item and either try to make a word out of it, or just remember the letters. The letters will trigger the memory of the item.

3. *Make Lists.* One sure way to remember things is to write things down. Of course, it's pretty important that you put the list somewhere where you know you will see it.

4. *Practice.* A common way to keep the brain cells rejuvenated is to practice memorizing. Give yourself little challenges every day to remember. Remember names, poetry, numbers, verses, or songs.

## Stay Competent

Another way to keep the brain cells active is to grow and stay competent in our areas of skill and expertise. I had friends who were in their 90's. Every morning Owen would read the newspaper from cover to cover for Edla and they would discuss the world's events. They wrote every day in journals, telling stories and commenting on politics, social and religious issues. It was never boring being in their presence because they usually knew more about current events than I did.

## Capitalize on Internal Creativity

Another way to stimulate the mind is to allow your innate curiosity to guide you into areas of personal creativity. According to the dictionary, to create is to "cause to come into being; as something unique that would not naturally evolve or that is not made by ordinary processes. It evolves from a person's own thought or imagination, as a work of art, an invention, to perform for the first time, to be the cause or occasion of, or to give rise to."

This definition implies that creativity must come from some thought or idea that is original. This is not necessarily true. Today, there really is not much that is original. Creativity is also the ability to use what already exists and manifest something out of it with your own intellect, experiences and imagination.

No matter what your age or place in life, you can access your own creativity because everyone is creative. Julia Cameron who wrote *The Artist's Way*, says that she has come to believe that creativity is our true nature; the reason why we struggle with our creativity is because we have blocks to it. She gives many suggestions and insight into how to expand our ability to be creative. Sark who wrote the *Inspiration Sandwich,* also has many good ideas to access our own ability to be creative.

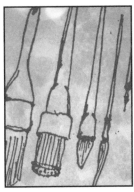

For many of us since childhood creativity has been culled out of us to make us seem more like everyone else. Even when we were asked in school to write an original story, or create a science project, we risked being ostracized by our fellow students if we were too creative. Because we feared rejection we did not want to stand out. (I don't remember originality or creativity being valued by teachers.) Somehow those experiences stay with us and we suppress our creative abilities. When this happens our own sense of adventure, exploration and creativity becomes stifled or nonexistent.

### Practice Creating

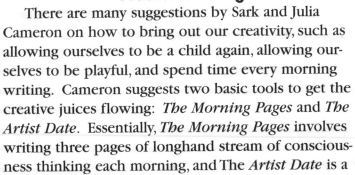

There are many suggestions by Sark and Julia Cameron on how to bring out our creativity, such as allowing ourselves to be a child again, allowing ourselves to be playful, and spend time every morning writing. Cameron suggests two basic tools to get the creative juices flowing: *The Morning Pages* and *The Artist Date*. Essentially, *The Morning Pages* involves writing three pages of longhand stream of consciousness thinking each morning, and The *Artist Date* is a block of time that we set aside for ourselves every week to nurture our creative consciousness. Essentially, it is time we set aside to play anyway we want to. It is a time when our analytical mind takes a rest and the creative, playful mind gets our nurturing love and attention.

If we are really interested in tapping into our creativity, another very helpful exercise is to read *Inspiration Sandwich* and do at least three things Sark suggests.

Being creative doesn't mean that we have to fancy ourselves as an artist, writer or poet. There are many ways to be creative:

**At work:**
1, Create a new program or better way of doing things.
2. Create a budget that meets your needs without cutting programs.

3. Restructure your workday or office

**At home:**

1. Design a new game for your children
2. Plan a trip
3. Decorate your home
4. Create a new menu

There are probably many other ways you can think of to create, play and let your mind explore itself. Make yourself a promise to set aside a minimum amount of time every week to be creative and make that time for yourself non-negotiable. Remember, we are focusing on keeping the mind stimulated and exercised so it will stay healthy.

**References:** Cameron, Julia. *The Artist's Way.* A must book for everyone to learn to tap into our own ability to be creative.

Restak, Richard M. *The Mind.* Very comprehensive insight into the working of the mind.

Weil, Andrew. *The Natural Mind.* Different approach to understanding the mind from a more holistic approach.

Sark. *Inspiration Sandwich.* Great whimsical book with good advice. Her journaling book is also quite good.

Moyers, Bill. *Healing and the Mind.* A great book based on the PBS series.

# HEALING RELATIONSHIPS
## Stress Reduction in Relationships

*"Treat your friends as you do your pictures,*
*and place them in their best light."*
Jennie Jerome Churchill

*"Life is partly what we make it, and partly*
*what it is made by the friends whom we choose."*
Tehyi Hseih

*"Inspiring people are vitamins for our spirits.*
*They come in all kinds of disguises and descriptions.*
*If you open your heart to being inspired,*
*they will appear."*
Sark

Remember writing down the five most important people in your life? Do you spend quality time with those people? As is true in any area of life, if we want something to grow and flourish, we must attend to it, be mindful and vigilant of it, care for it, and nourish it. What must we do to preserve and grow the relationships that are important to us?

Relationships are the foundation of our existence whether it is professional, casual or intimate. We use relationships for many things—for defining ourselves, for comfort, for stability, for validation, for a sense of meaning. We express our essence, grow and learn when we are in relationships with others.

Although we all have relationships, they can sure be complicated and complex. They are sometimes the source of our greatest exhilaration and our greatest stress, bringing bliss one minute or frustration and anxiety the next. In all of my years of coaching, counseling or observing others in relationships, as well as in my own relationships, it seems we usually get stressed because of some perception we have about how we relate with others.

Remember the iceberg analogy from Chapter 2? What we see, say and do on the surface of our relationships is not necessarily what we want or expect from others underneath the surface. On the surface we use acceptable social practices and language with each other, but if we put on our scuba gear and go underneath the surface we may discover that the expectations we have of others are not being met. Do I believe you see me as worthwhile? (self-esteem) Do I feel intimidated or insecure with you? (security) Do I believe you think I'm not good enough in a particular area? (competency) Do I believe I can trust you or that you trust me? (trust) Do I believe you really love or like me? (love).

When we are in a relationship together, it helps to see what needs we both bring to the relationship and how the expectations we have of each other might be causing each of us stress.

There are many people in our lives who are important to us and we want to spend time with each of them. In my profession, I see men and women who live with constant guilt about how much time they don't spend with their children or spouse. Sometimes the people at work know us better than our families. Sometimes the daycare provider knows our children better than we do.

I always felt guilty for not spending enough time with my children when they were growing up. Since the experts always say that it's the quality of time spent with children that counts, I tried to make sure that when I was with them, I was with them. In fact, when they were in elementary school, my daughter, Heidi, said to me one day, "I wish you were like other mothers and were home when we got home from school and had cookies and milk for us." That comment hurt deeply because there was no way it would ever happen. I was convinced that I was damaging my children. One day, some years later, we were preparing for a trip to a dude ranch in Montana. In the midst of all the hullabaloo of packing and getting ready, I realized I had forgotten to get us something to eat. We poured ourselves in the van and hurried over to Wendy's to eat. While sitting there, Heidi said, "Do you remember, Mom, when I said I wish you were like the other mothers? Well, I'm glad you're not. I really like the life we have because we have fun." I realized once again that the experts are right. It's the quality of time we spend with our children that counts. And the same is true for other family members and friends.

Without making ourselves more stressed, how can we manage all of the relationships in our lives? One suggestion is to make a list starting with those who are closest to us and then others who are important to nurture on an ongoing basis. Start by examining our monthly calendar. Crossing off the times that are occupied with work, exercising and special appointments with ourselves, write in times to be with our children and close family members. Set aside certain times of the week that are given only to our children, if they are still at home; that, then, becomes non-negotiable. Set times with your spouse or significant other. That, too, becomes non-negotiable. We must treat these times as appointments that cannot be broken except in extreme emergencies. Then we can look at other ways and times to connect with our friends and other family members.

**JUNE**

**3 Mon**
7:00 Exercise
8:30 Staff Mtg
10:00 Team Meeting
12:00 Lunch w/Brad
5:30 Family time
10:00 - 10:15 Quiet Time

**4 Tue**
7:30 Breakfast w/Jill
12:00 Lunch Pick up laundry
6:00 Italian Class
10:00 - 10:15 Quiet time

**5 Wed**
7:00 Exercise
1:00 Customer Support Meeting
5:30 Family time
10:00 - 10:15 quiet time

**6 Thur**
7:00 Exercise
12:00 Lunch errands
2:30 Meeting with supervisor
6:00 Class
10:00 - 10:15 Quiet time

**7 Fri**
10:00 Team Meeting
12:00 Lunch; write emails to friends
5:00 Meet friends for FAC

**8 Sat**
9:00 exercise/shopping
10:00 Soccer/Ballet
Clean House
Date w/Spouse

**9 Sun**
Sleep Late
Family time
Take Walk
Evening Quiet time

# LIVING LOVE

It is also very difficult to learn to love someone if we never spend time with them. Make it a point to spend 15 minutes each day of uninterrupted time with the people closest to us. It is most important that the people we love know we are really with them. Sometimes it may be tedious. Maybe your child loves the zoo and you would rather be sitting on the porch swing. Maybe your spouse likes to walk and you would rather be fly fishing. Loving means giving up what you want to do at times in order to please and share time with those you love.

There are many ways, as well, to let others know how much they are loved. Saying "I love you" should never be undermined or dismissed. Sending cards, flowers, giving little gifts are some of the most common ways to share our feelings. My oldest daughter, Renny, tells me many times a week how much she loves and appreciates me, and when she also sends a beautiful card with the same message, it still touches me.

Everyone needs hugs. We must never forget to touch others, and when appropriate, to say "I love you."

Other ideas are:

- Surprise someone with something they really like for no reason at all.
- Leave love notes on their pillows, lunch sacks, plates, or someplace where they will find them later.
- Send emails with just a note of love or appreciation.
- Even though you don't want to, do something they want to do.
- Send a card with a little note telling them how you feel about them.
- Treat them with the same respect you would treat the person you admire most in the world if that person were in your home right now.
- Listen with your whole presence while they are talking with you.

- Know what matters to them.
- Pray for them.

## Romantic Love

Even though Valentine's Day is highly commercialized, it still holds an important thought. If we want to be loved, we need to love. We have already learned that love is a need. When was the last time you told the most important person in your life: "I really love you!" and meant it? When was the last time you really had a "love in?" Making love is not just sex. In fact sex is a very small part of it. Making love is something that occurs every day. It is engaging in the act of love making by being kind, gentle and thoughtful to each other. There are many ways to "make love."

## Importance of Romance

Many men are resistant to romance because it appears to be hard work and takes too much time. Real joy occurs in a relationship when the other person is pleased and content. Romance really means taking the time to please our partner. What are the things that please our partner? What is the "foreplay" that is needed to heighten the pleasure between us? This definition of foreplay is not just sexual acts, but the "dance" that occurs between two lovers which may culminate in a sexual act. It may be something as simple as holding hands in the grocery store, smiling "that smile," a soft touch or hug, the endearing names we call each other—anything that says, "you're special."

There are many ways to be romantic. Overall, whatever way we use, remember that tenderness, kindness, and gentleness are at the core. It is saying in many different ways: "I really love you."

- Leave love post-it notes where your partner will find it when you're not there.
- Kissing gently, holding, and touching softly in passing.
- Wear provocative undergarments.
- Eat and bathe by candlelight.
- Dance together alone in silky pajamas.

- Do something outrageous or shocking, like putting a special message or article of clothing in a lunch box.
- Be creative and have fun together.

Playing with people we love is also important, as is eating, laughing, and crying with them. The overarching theme is that to show another our love for them means that we set ourselves aside to be attentive to, and to be truly with, that person. This does not imply that we become like door mats and relinquish our own sense of worth. Nor does it mean we are held hostage to another's needs. It means that when we love, we give of who we are, as well as attend to and affirm our partners.

## HOUSEHOLD CALENDARS

Many families use a family calendar which is posted in a common area of the house where everyone can access it. They find it very helpful in identifying each family member's activities as well as family time together. It also helps to identify who is responsible for particular chores and other family responsibilities. This kind of organization helps to give a sense of control to all of the activities that families are involved in today. And, thank goodness for email and voice mail! It may not be the same as a face-to-face interaction, but it helps in keeping touch with those we care about.

## DAILY CHATS

One of my favorite things to do is to perform marriage ceremonies. I spend time counseling with the couple ahead of time to talk through everything from what are the most difficult issues between them to where do they want the attendants to stand during the ceremony. I enjoy basking in the love and commitment the couple shares. Later, when I see the same couple I am always amazed that often the warm glow of the relationship has become a cold frost. What happened? Why have starter marriages become an accepted phenomenon in our society? Too often our days go by one by one without spending quality time with the people most important to us, especially those with whom we live. It is important for us to make a pact with our children and spouse/significant other to spend at least 15 minutes every day to just visit—to just be together.

It has been said that the best gift you can give anyone is rapt attention. This is particularly true of our spouse/significant other or children. This should be time without telephones or television. Use the time to talk about good things, funny things that happened during the day, or share thoughts, hopes and dreams. Try not to dwell on negative things and worries. Use the time to talk about the meaningful things we love about each other.

I knew a couple that had a martini together alone every evening while the husband read poetry to his wife. They had nine children who knew that the time their parents spent every day together was sacred and woe to anyone who bothered them. I loved being around them because they always seemed to have a rich and deep love for each other.

## RESOLVE CONFLICT APPROPRIATELY

Unresolved conflict with the most important people in our lives is the surest way to destroy a relationship. Yet, having the courage to be honest about hurts with those we love is the most difficult thing many of us have to do. Why is it so difficult to tell the people we love that we are hurt, or that we disagree with them? It is true that once words are spoken, we can never take them back. We must learn how to say the words in such a way that it keeps everyone's integrity and dignity intact. It has always been known that the surest sign of a dysfunctional relationship is if each of the parties keeps secrets from the other. I mentioned earlier how my daughter, Heidi, cannot be inauthentic. Because of Heidi's commitment to honesty and bringing everything out in the open, my other daughter, Renny, also, is committed to honesty and openness. It has created a kind of purity in our family environment that helps our relationships to be stress free.

When I have counseled couples I have found that there are three things that cause stress and conflict in a marriage—children, finances and sex. Before we go to sleep at night, it is important that we clear the air of hurts with the people we love. Even the Bible says we should not to let the sun go down on our anger. (Ephesians 4:26) Sleep and rest are hard to come by when we are full of negative energy. It is particularly important with children that they do not believe their parents are angry with them or with each other when they go to bed. We need to create warmth, care and lovingness with all of our important "others" before we put our head on the pillow to sleep.

If you have a hard time being honest about your feelings with important people, go back to Chapter 5 and revisit how to express yourself to people without causing unnecessary strain, tension and stress.

### Helping Children Express Themselves

Many years ago I was a child therapist for very disturbed children. Although they may have had a psychological diagnosis, they were just like other children in their inability to really talk about what bothered them. We found that the best outlet for these children to express themselves was to play—whether it was playing with each other, with toys or just drawing pictures. I was so impressed with the power of playing that I used the same technique with my own children when they were hurt or angry.

All children need some kind of outlet to say they hurt or are frightened. The number one standard for allowing children to express themselves is just that: allow children to express. The question for many parents is how that expression manifests itself. Along with toys and drawing a picture, other ways to help express hurt and anger are to allow children to act out their story or use a method where you might begin a story and your children fill in the blanks.

Children aren't the only ones who have difficulty expressing themselves appropriately. Teenagers struggle with how to relate hurt and anger as well. As parents it's so important to pay attention and really listen to our children and teenagers by keeping our own mouth shut. Allow them to talk to us without telling them how they should think or feel.

After the Columbine High School tragedy, many counselors were called to work through the grief and fear with not only the Columbine students, but students around the world. I was continually shocked at how many teenagers stated they never show their true feelings with their parents or talk about things that are really bothering them. The common theme was, "Why should I, they don't listen, they don't care. All they want to do is tell me what they want me to do and make me listen to them because they don't really care what I think or feel." I know you hear, as I do, the hurt in that statement. Our kids need us to pay attention, to really listen and try to understand how they see things from their perspective. Unfortunately, too many times we want to control them.

## LET GO OF CONTROL

When we think about it, most of the heartburn we incur in our lives with people is because we can't get them to do what we want them to do. Don't they know that we are wiser, smarter, more experienced than they and that if only they would do what we think is best they would be so much happier? Sometimes, it's true that if they followed our advice, they might be better off. But if it's important to them, they'll get there on their own. It is so hard for us to "let go."

Letting go also means that I: 1) let go of trying to control other people and things (like the weather, traffic, news reports, company policy) and 2) accept people and things for who and what they are. We do not have control over other people (of any age). We may influence others and events, but we cannot control them. There are enough things in ourselves that are difficult to control—our thinking, our emotions, diseases, and body structure.

It is very important that we learn to accept the things in others that we cannot change and learn to find things about them that make them valuable to us.

Sometimes our need to control others comes from our need to have power over them. As history has repeated over and over, individuals or groups who take it upon themselves to exert power over others are probably weak and insecure themselves. Whenever we try to control others, we place ourselves in a fearful situation. We live in constant fear that the other person might find a way to usurp our power and control. This begins a never-ending cycle where we try to wield more and more power over other individuals or groups to fortify their subservience to us and the control we believe we have over them. Those of us who have been in this cycle know only too well how seductive this thinking is and fraught with anxiety, stress and disappointments.

The way we control others can be very obvious or very subtle. People control others by giving or withholding money, withholding love or demanding attention. I know many older parents who control their adult children through weak health and/or guilt.

The way we can stop the cycle is to first recognize it. The second step is to just stop it!

- Stop telling people we care about what to do and how to do it.
- Stop giving people our opinions, unless asked.
- Stop using tears, orders, commands, threats or self-destructive behavior to make others feel guilty to get the behaviors we want.
- Stop making value judgments about others—any others.
- Stop acting as though our lives will end if that other person does not do what we desire.
- Stop trying to live our life through another.
- Stop blaming others for our lives.

If we have engaged in any one of these behaviors, it may be difficult to stop. It takes a great amount of self talk to understand that we may be guilty of trying to control others, and it also takes a great amount of self talk to stop that behavior.

If we, as parents, find it hard to let go of controlling our children, we need to ask ourselves, "What need is missing for me? Why do I need to cling? Is it because my own self-esteem is wrapped up in my children? Are my children the gratification of my security? Does it have something to do with my competency as a parent? Is it because I crave love from them?" Once we get to the bottom of our own needs, we can begin to work on that and let our children find their own way.

If we are the recipient of controlling behavior, it is important first to recognize it, then ask why we allow that person to control us. Why have we given that person power over us? Again, to deal with it, review the techniques in Chapter 5, "Healing the Emotional." Accept loved ones for who they are NOW, not what you want them to be

Another great stressor is the frustration we experience in trying to attempt to make others into the people we want them to be. Husbands and wives do this to each other. When people marry, they believe that they will be able to train or remake their spouse into what they want and when the change does not occur, it causes frustration and anger. If we are courting someone with the idea of eventually living with that person or marrying them, it is important to realize that we cannot change them. They must want to change. If we cannot tolerate who they are RIGHT NOW, then it is not a good idea to plan living a life with them. The hidden agenda of one spouse trying to change the other, or not loving them for who they are right now, does not bode well for a happy marriage or relationship.

It is also important to understand and accept that when a loved one is engaged in behavior that is destructive, we cannot control him or her. At what point do we let go of control over a child or loved one when we know their behavior is self-destructive? Although the realization is difficult, no one can impose change or control on another and expect the change to be effective. The individual must want the change, seek the change and be committed to it. The question is, can we love that person for who he or she is intrinsically? Or do we just love the person for how they make us look or feel?

A woman who had two sons confided to me that one has always been her favorite and the other she has always been somewhat ashamed of. No one ever knew how she felt about her boys but she said she never wanted to take the one son anywhere. To her he was unattractive and unpleasant which, she believed, cast a negative image on her. When the boys were in high school, the mother and father divorced. The boy who was her favorite and fulfilled her ego needs, went to live with his father, by choice, and rarely came to see her. The other boy stayed with his mother, by choice, and now often stops by to check on her. At the time I talked with her, she was still struggling with the guilt of her lack of loving feelings about her son. Too often we use our children as a means to build our own egos rather than seeing them, accepting them and loving them for who they are.

### Allow Interruptions

We will constantly be interrupted in our personal and work life. Learn that interruptions are part of your "job" as a worker, parent, friend, or family member. One way to control interruptions is to put time frames around them. For example, when a family member or friend calls, limit the call. When children interrupt, be focused on the request, respond to the issue and then excuse yourself to get back to whatever you were doing. At work, if possible, monitor the time necessary to respond to the interruption, make a note of where you left off, then excuse yourself. Generally, we know intuitively when the cause of the interruption has been answered and you can go back to your task. We become agitated when we feel powerless. If you take charge of the interruption, answer the request, respond to the problem, and give the necessary attention, it will help resolve the sense of helplessness and frustration at being interrupted.

# CULTIVATE RELATIONSHIPS

The old saying is, "If we want to have friends, we need to be one!" What does it mean to be friendly? How do we cultivate friendships?

When I was growing up, the way we kept in touch with friends and family was by writing letters or driving over for a visit. Every Sunday, my dad would drive us to someone's home to visit, or people would come to our house. Sometimes we stopped at two or three homes to stay long enough for the adults to have a cup of coffee, catch up on the gossip, and then we would be off again until the next time. The coffeepot was always on at our house, too, in case visitors decided to come. I used to sit on the floor watching everyone's hands "talking" a mile a minute and was fascinated at the way relationships were developed and nurtured. In my young mind, I was impressed with how important it is to keep in touch with friends and family. Whenever we piled in the car to go on to the next place or home, my parents' spirits were considerably lifted and happy. I was aware how much I, too, looked forward to these visits.

We all want and need to keep in touch with loved ones. We become anxious and guilty when days and weeks go by without a "touch." Often, the reason we do not keep in touch is because we don't want to take an enormous amount of time from our busy schedules to write long letters or have long phone conversations. Most of us work long hours, have required tasks to attend to when we come home and then fall into bed at night exhausted. It doesn't take long before we feel alienated from the ones who mean the most to us.

Hopefully, we're all on the internet. A lot of positive and negative things have been said about email. We can make it work well for us by spending time often checking in on friends. Even though our mail may be short, it lets our loved ones know we're thinking of them. Why not get a digital camera making a special point to take pictures to share online? It's easy to make copies and keep them handy. Purchase a box of nice stationery cards with the list of addresses of our family and friends close by. Keep a book of stamps in the card box. Whenever we think of that individual, take out a card, write a few words, enclose a picture and send it on its way. It will only take a few minutes.

A sure way to make friends is to be friendly. Someone once said that the shortest distance between two strangers is a smile. Smiling is the first rule of being friendly. The other is paying attention and listening. If you are one of those people who find it difficult to engage in dialogue and conversation with others, practice the art of visiting. Have several questions handy to engage others in conversation. Use questions with which you are comfortable and practice with people who are close to you.

Listening is also important. Look people in the eye, and nod when you agree. Ask for clarification when you don't understand. If you don't agree it's not necessary to argue or become combative. You can say, "that's an interesting perspective," "I've never thought of that before" or, "I don't believe I agree with you, but it's an interesting thought." It keeps the conversation going without being critical or argumentative.

### Learn the Art of Entertaining

 Entertaining is a wonderful way to let friends and family know how much you care. There are many ways to entertain. Dinner parties and cocktail parties are the most common. And, there are always excuses to have one: A sports event, a holiday, a birthday, or other special event. The important thing to remember is that it does not have to be fancy. What matters is that we have good food, friends and a little music. The rest takes care of itself.

If you find it difficult to cook for people, ask everyone to bring a dish and you provide the place. People who love you don't care if they have to bring a dish. There are many cookbooks and entertainment books at the bookstores, so find two or three dinners that are easy to fix and you know you can count on. Then entertain away! When I started out having dinner parties, I had two or three standbys of every course that never failed.

Try to have a dinner party every three months and gather people together that you believe will stimulate a good conversation. I have friends who think about their dinner guests in terms of how much they would enjoy each other. When people arrive, they share what might be interesting to the others to help the guests find a common ground. If you are anxious about the conversation, plan ahead of time what questions you might ask or topics you might introduce to stimulate conversation. Always plug into what people are interested in. Try to stay away from conversations that might be potentially argumentative like politics or religion. People like to talk about themselves and what they are doing, so encourage people to talk about themselves. The mark of a great entertainer is someone who helps other people enjoy themselves.

It's also important to have special events with your family. Make a point to have candlelight dinners often. In fact, I read recently that a study showed that when family members, especially children, eat by candlelight, it makes dinnertime more calming, relaxing and less stressful. Use the best china, silver and crystal with a table cloths and flowers. It doesn't matter what the food is, it always is festive when it's on the best dishes. Other ideas include having fun nights when the food may just be hot dogs or pizza, but everyone has to wear a special goofy hat, or clown noses, or costumes. Make dinner time the most fun part of the day with celebration or romance.

## OKAY TO SAY "NO"

The hardest thing to do with people who are special to us is to tell them "no." Many times stressful situations are caused because we think the way to please everyone is by doing everything they ask. There are times when we must "just say no" in order to take care of ourselves.

### Saying "No" to Our Parents

As parents age certain needs become more prominent. Parents want and need to be wanted and needed. For many aging parents, the sense of not being productive or vital is cause for depression and sadness. If they become more demanding of their children's time and attention, this may, in turn, cause great guilt in adult children because we already have many demands in our own lives that require our attention. Balance is the key. I remember a woman coming to me after one of my speeches saying that her stress had become unbearable because of the guilt she felt with her parents. They both were in a nursing home and they were very demanding of her time. If she didn't go to see them or call at least once a day, she felt guilty. It finally was consuming her life. As she stood there with tears in her eyes, I asked her, "What would happen if you told them you could not come every day?" Her fear was that they would stop loving her. When she realized that would never happen, she left with some ideas about how she would manage the time she spent with her parents and still have time for herself and her family.

### Saying "No" to Our Children

Children at every age make many demands on their parents. I am sure you can tell me stories about parents who almost kill themselves giving up their lives to please or satisfy their children. Many parents believe their children won't love them if they don't get all of the "stuff" they want. My experience is that children need and want love. If they know we love them, then even though they may be disappointed that we can't provide them with everything they want, when we say "no" they will still love us.

### Saying "No" to Our Spouse/Significant Other

We also feel guilty and stressed when we say "no" to our spouse or significant other. There are times when it is important to maintain our own will in a situation. I have a friend who was totally in love with her husband. She adored him. Whatever he wanted, she would accommodate. As she got older, she began to realize that she had no real understanding of herself. She measured everything about her in relationship to what her husband thought, what he wanted, and how he wanted her to be. It was an amazing thing to watch when within a very short period of time she realized she had no idea who she really was. She then became angry, not only at him but at herself.

If we do not feel like making love, if we do not want to engage in certain activities, it is important that we honor ourselves by saying "no." This seems particularly hardest in the act of love making. I was amazed at how many times "the bed" came up during counseling couples and the high degree of stress it causes in a relationship. Many women believe that having sex is a duty and therefore, do it reluctantly or grudgingly. Others want to enjoy sex but find it unsatisfying. If this situation continues, sex is a dread rather than desired and will become a wedge between the couple. If you do not feel like engaging in love making, tell your spouse "not tonight" or "not now." Make sure you let your spouse know that it is not about him or her—it's about how you are feeling at that moment, and that it doesn't mean you will never want it with him or her. He or she will still love you even though it might embarrass them or hurt them at that moment. It is helpful to talk to each other about ways that we can both say "no" without internalizing it and believing that the relationship is damaged in some way.

If the desire is never there, please get counseling or help for yourself. If the way love making occurs is distasteful to either party, it's important to talk it out and get it resolved. Making love is a sensitive area that can become volatile, so if there is a problem it's important to share these feelings, read helpful books, or get counseling.

### Saying "No" to Our Friends

Friendships are supposed to be mutually gratifying and fun. I know people who struggle with some friends because those friends have become so intrusive in their lives. Jenny Churchill said, "People are friends in spots." I believe that we have longtime or forever friends and then good friends that we have met along the way that were friends "in that spot." Just because we don't want to be with those former friends now, doesn't mean the relationship wasn't meaningful at the time.

So often we get stressed and feel guilty because we don't give every one of our friends our total attention all the time. In our desire to maintain friends, it is often hard to tell them "no" when we don't want to do something, or want to make other plans. It is important to understand that we don't have to tell anyone what our other plans are. We can just say "I've made other plans, or commitments." The hardest thing about saying "no" to people who are close to us is that they often expect a forthcoming explanation. Many times they want to examine whether our plans are really more important than spending time with them. It's important to remember that we do not have to share with people what our other commitments are. If that person is truly our friend they may be momentarily hurt because they want to be with us, but they will still love us.

The most important thing to remember is to keep balance. Balance our time with our family, friends and significant other, as well as all of the other important areas of our lives.

## GET OUT OF TOXIC RELATIONSHIPS

Many years ago, I was in a very destructive and abusive relationship. The man was mentally, emotionally and verbally abusive. Every day I knew how toxic and destructive the relationship was, but somehow I was so intimidated by him that I couldn't get him out of my life. For any of you who are in a similar situation, I know you will understand! My friends and family would shake their heads and wonder what was wrong with me that I couldn't "throw the bum out." I lived in constant embarrassment and stress—knowing how stupid I was for staying with him, yet I was too intimidated to get rid of him.

Finally, with great trepidation and desperation, I called the movers and in one day packed up all of his stuff, changed the locks and moved his belongings to storage. Even though he harassed me after that, my situation turned out well. I know that many other men and women get harassed, stalked, hurt and even killed because of a deranged or toxic spouse or significant other. These relationships cause enormous stress.

Toxic relationships sap energy, destroy the spirit and are incredibly anxiety producing. If you find yourself in a toxic relationship or are involved in doing toxic things to yourself, it is important for spirit healing that you remove yourself as quickly as possible from the situation. You know you are in a toxic relationship when you seem drained of energy, get depressed easily, find yourself becoming more and more negative in the presence of that individual, or dread being in that person's presence. If you believe you are in a toxic relationship, it is important to get help to get out of it. If the toxic person is a spouse or living companion and it is difficult to get out of the relationship immediately, find time every day to be alone and away from that person. In the meantime, find someone to counsel with to help you get the strength to get away from the person permanently.

What are some of the things you can do while you are in the midst of a toxic relationship?

- Set aside some alone time each day to nurture yourself. It may be engaging in a hobby that is important to you, reading a book, watching a favorite movie, taking a hot bubble bath, taking a long walk. Make sure you do something special for yourself every day.

- Write out your feelings on a pad of paper as often as you can. When you are through writing tear the paper up and throw it away. Keep writing until all the hurt and venom is released so you can deal with your situation more appropriately.

- Read books that help you gain the strength to make changes in your life.

- Find ways to bring humor into your life. (See section on humor, page 82.)

- Cultivate friendships that nourish you. You must be careful, however, not to spend too much time discussing your toxic relationship with your friends. They can become frustrated in listening to us, particularly if we do nothing about it. Usually friends will be most helpful if they know we intend to make a change in our lives.

- Go away to the ocean or mountains by yourself for a few days to be alone and do something to nourish your spirit. In the end, however, it is important that you get the help you need to get out of a relationship that is poisoning you.

# DELEGATE

As most people who delegate know, sometimes it is easier to do things yourself than to delegate responsibilities to others. Part of juggling and balancing is sharing responsibilities not only at work, but also at home.

### Delegating with Children

One of lessons that children learn is that parents have chores too. So when the list of chores is made, make sure that every family member is listed. Sometimes it is helpful to negotiate chores among family members on a weekly or monthly basis. This takes the burden off of one parent who might be responsible for the lion's share of the load. Children do enjoy a variety of tasks, even being responsible for challenging jobs like cooking dinner. In fact, dinner time can be a time of fun, in spite of the chaos, when everyone has a specific part and/or task. Allowing family members to be creative as to who does what can create a great sense of purpose and importance in the family. If you are compulsive and think it is too much trouble to have certain tasks done by the children, learn to let it go by practicing with little changes first.

### Delegating in a Home Without Children

Many of us believe that only homes with children should have a clear delegation of tasks. If both partners work, it is important that the at-home work be shared. If one person keeps the checkbook, the other can write the checks and pay the bills. If one cooks, the other can clean up. If one cleans the bathrooms, the other can clean the garage. It is helpful to vary the tasks by taking turns.

We can also develop a reward system for ourselves. If we both finish our tasks by a certain time, we can reward ourselves with a treat that is meaningful to both of us. Make the time doing a tedious chore fun. For example, play dance music, listen to a tape of a comedian, wear costumes, or funny hats. Many people, (single, roommates or couples) I have met say they look forward to Saturday or "chore" time because they put on their favorite music as loud as they can and sing or dance through their chores.

In thinking about the quality of relationships with those who are important in our lives, it is once again most important to remember that their spirit needs—self-esteem, security, competency, trust and love—are just like ours. Stresses usually come in relationships when we ignore those needs in ourselves and others.

**References:** There are many books that give helpful suggestions on all of the subjects discussed in this chapter. I encourage you to pick out the area or areas that are the most troubling to you and find resources that will help you with these issues.

Gray, John. *Men Are From Mars, Women Are From Venus.* All of John Gray's books are helpful in understanding relationships.

Fine, Debra. *Fine Art of Small Talk.* Wonderful and helpful book to learn conversational skills.

# 9 HEALING THE CAREER
## Stress Reducers in Careers

*Every calling is great when greatly pursued.*
Oliver Wendell Holmes

*The bottom line is that I am responsible for my own well-being,
my own happiness. The choices and decisions I make regarding
my life directly influence the quality of my days.*
Kathleen Andrus

*Slow down and enjoy life. It's not only the scenery you miss by
going too fast—you also miss the sense of where you are going,
and why.*
Eddie Cantor

Today, as I sit down to write, a very close friend has been fired.
It was all part of a merger. He had several clues it was coming:

phone calls were not returned, he was left out of
meetings and not included in inner-circle lunch-
eons. Still, when the shoe dropped, he was
stunned. The new owner/managers are younger,
faster and more energetic than my 45 year old
friend. This dehumanizing scenario is repeated hundreds of times every day in corporations and businesses across the United States. The mantra is: "no
hard feelings, nothing personal, it's strictly business." In the frenzied activity to position organizations for Wall Street, company managers try to find
ways to make shareholders happy at the expense of making the
employees of the company happy. On the one hand, the underly-
ing message is that people are just parts of a machine so that
when they get old or useless, they are set aside. On the other,
companies try to obtain and retain employees who are perceived
to be the best and brightest.

Workers have more to do, less time and energy in which to do it, and no certainty that their jobs are secure. As workers become stressed and personally less productive, they negatively impact other workers, costing the organization in sick days, increased insurance premiums and the cost of hiring and training new staff. The World Labor Report, published annually by the United Nations, states that the number one issue confronting the world's worker is stress and burnout. Each year, in the United States alone, over $200 billion is spent on costs associated with stress and burnout. Worker's compensation claims total over $187 billion per year. Injuries and accidents are primarily caused when people are preoccupied due to stress-related problems. Educational institutions report that the symptoms of stress are apparent at all grade levels.

No one needs to remind us that our jobs can be our greatest source of stress. We constantly live with the stresses of the economic pressures affecting whether we have jobs, and, much of the reason for our distress at work is that what we do seems so discordant with what gives us pleasure and meaning. In my consulting, training and speaking over the years, I have heard many stories of people who are trying to keep themselves whole by finding some kind of meaning in jobs that are perceived as not meaningful or fulfilling. I am amazed at how no one dreads retirement. Everyone wants to retire. Why? So we can do what we want. So we can choose a career or calling that is meaningful to us.

## Is My Work Meaningful?

Survey data from the Department of Labor shows, overwhelmingly, that employees look for and value the following top five elements at work:

1. **That *my* work and *the* work are meaningful**—It is important that we know that the work we do is meaningful and that the company we work for does meaningful work.

2. **I am recognized and thanked for the work I do and the contribution I make**—It is important to not only be recognized for a job well done or be thanked for making a contribution by our boss or the company, it is also nice to be recognized by our peers.

3. **That I get support in terms of the resources needed to do my work**—It is incredibly important to have the right tools and technology to do your work well.

4. **That I have opportunities to grow and develop**—Not only is training important, but being with people who are considered the benchmarks or perform their jobs with excellence is important to our learning and development. We need to learn in order to continue to be motivated to do our jobs.

5. **That I am paid fairly.**

   Notice that the number one value employees look for is knowing their work is meaningful.

Making a contribution to life is ultimately important for all of us. We seek meaning in many ways—through our contributions to our family, church, volunteer organizations and friendships. Some may seek meaning through material possessions. Many of us never think of finding meaningfulness in work or think of our jobs as a career or a calling. We think of our jobs as a means to get money to support what we do outside of work. Yet what we do in our careers, professional life and work supports our belief that we are doing something meaningful in our lives.

Do we look forward to the work we do? Do we believe we are making a meaningful contribution? Do we believe that others are impacted by our work? If we cannot find meaningfulness in our work, we are easily stressed and will soon burn out.

How on earth could anyone find something meaningful in his or her work unless it was for a totally altruistic purpose? Discovering that the work itself is important helps us learn how to manage the stress *of* work and *at* work. This change of perception is the beginning of taking control of ourselves. I believe that any work we do is meaningful. It's the way we think about its

value that matters. If I clean toilets, haul garbage, sell groceries, or conduct heart surgery, in some way it is all meaningful. It's important that I know that the work I do contributes to the well being of others.

In what way does the work you do and the organization you work for contribute to the community or society? Clearly hold your organization's mission in front of you to help remind you that you are part of a team that does important work. The first step is to know that your organization does meaningful work... and then, how about you? The second step is to discover how to live your mission through the work you do. In considering your relationship to your work, are you living your own mission?

## WHAT IS MY LIFE MISSION?

Defining a mission statement is not just for your organization. Many of you may believe that you don't need to know what your life mission is; that being a parent or good citizen is enough. And, that is certainly admirable. However, have you ever thought that your life seemed to lack direction? That you were just going through the motions of every day living? That there was something you were missing? That you could be doing more or contributing more? Knowing your life mission or purpose is not about the roles you perform, like parenting, being an engineer, an assistant, doctor, or student. It is about who you are.

What is the deepest longing in your heart that seeks accomplishment or achievement? No matter how hard you try, what is it that you cannot help yourself from doing? What do you always go back to? What is that deepest part of you that must express itself? Is it teaching? Is it caretaking others? Is it fixing things? Is it curiosity about how things work? Is it in finding solutions? Once you discover your basic essence, you are better able to develop a mission statement that makes sense.

When you write your mission statement, it is helpful to start by using the following model: My mission (or purpose) is to _____(verb or verbs)_____(outcome)_____ for _____(recipient)_____.

Laurie Beth Jones, author of the book, *The Path: Creating Your Mission Statement for Work and Life*, gives a very clear step-by-step process to developing your own mission statement.

Once you are clear about your mission, then you can ask yourself what would be the most natural pathway to express that essence? For example, if you always find yourself wanting to teach, coach or give advice, maybe your essence is in teaching. What can you do that will satisfy that essence? What are the kinds of jobs that would satisfy that essence? If you just can't help yourself from fixing things that are broken, then what would be the kinds of jobs that would satisfy you? If you want to fix things or change things that are in the world today, what would be the best avenue to make that happen? If you want to take care of others, what would be the best way to pursue that desire? When you have reflected on these questions, write down a statement that best captures that purpose.

## KNOW YOUR EXPECTATIONS

Most of my professional work involves helping organizations figure out and/or help fix what is keeping a group from working more productively together. I have found that the core of the problem is in the fact that people are not clear about expectations, both their's and others'. Taking it a step further, when we look at most relationships, whether it is with our family, spouse, significant other, co-workers, or boss, when things get stressful it's usually because one person didn't meet the expectations of the other.

There are some basic and fundamental mechanisms that need to be in place at work in order to reduce stress. As I already mentioned, it's important to know that we are working at something that is meaningful to us. Secondly, it's important to be very clear about what is expected of us by our boss and co-workers. Clarifying expectations in relationships is not a *once-and-for-all* proposition—sometimes it takes continual checking with our boss, our colleague, our teacher and even our spouse.

Most of us have a basic notion of what co-workers, bosses and loved ones expect from us. That's a good place to start. In order to make sure that expectations are being met, we must have conversations with the people involved. You may wonder, "How do I do it? How do I talk to my boss and co-workers about expectations without coming across as bossy, demanding or controlling?"

Sometimes we believe we are giving people the information, report or service they want and it is not meeting their needs. So the very first part of our discussion needs to confirm we are on the right track. The first thing we want to do is approach others in the spirit of helpfulness. Why? Because it will help defuse the defensiveness of others to engage in a conversation with us about expectations. Once we have clarified that we are providing what others want from us, we can engage them in a discussion about our own needs and wants in order for us to get our job done.

With co-workers and even family and friends, a way of opening the dialogue might be:

*Here is what I think you want or need from me. Or, I have been doing this, or providing this kind of information to you. Is this what you want or need? Is it enough? Is there anything more I can do for you that would be helpful?*

This tends to create a non-defensive environment. When you have cleared up what you can best do to help your co-worker, family or friends, it is easier to mention what your needs might be. For example:

*I appreciate the information you have been providing me thus far, and it would be even more helpful if I could ask you or count on you to provide further information in the following areas...*

The way to get at expectations you and others have of each other, it is helpful to diminish the defensiveness by starting out with how you want to meet their expectations more clearly.

Many employees have asked me how to get helpful feedback from their bosses. I have found in my many years of coaching and consulting that most bosses really are not sure any more than we are about what needs to be done and how it needs to be accomplished. Unfortunately, they are usually too vulnerable to admit it. One way we can become indispensable is to be proactive rather than passively wait for our boss to tell us what to do.

Once when I was consulting with a company, I was asked to coach a very bright young woman who had just been promoted to a vice president position. She was waiting for her boss (the CEO) to tell her what to do. The CEO, in the meantime, told me, "That's why I hired her. I expect her to know what to do. I'll tell her if it's not what I want." I have heard that line many, many times. It boils down to, "I don't know what I want, but I'll recognize it when I see it."

The following model will help to open up a conversation that can clarify expectations that bosses and co-workers have of us and we have of them:

**Here's what I've done thus far.**

or

**This is what I've accomplished to date.**

This lets our boss know the status of what we have done to the present time.

**Here is what I believe should be done next.**

or

**Here are some ideas of different options or alternatives.**

This lets our boss know we are thinking creatively about other options and alternatives.

**Here is what I believe the objective is,
or the desired outcome.**

This clarifies what is agreed upon as the desired outcome or end result that is being sought.

**What can I do to help you?**

or

**What do you need me to do in addition to
what I'm already doing?**

This has the effect of placing ourselves in a partnership role with our boss. It lets him or her know that we care about the work we do and are interested in making the department a success.

It is not necessary that these statements or questions be used exactly in the order written. Basically, we are making a point to clarify what is expected of us, and we are taking charge of our contribution to the organization. In order to do that, we must know and identify:

✔ What we have already accomplished,
✔ Other options or alternatives we may have considered,
✔ What we believe to be the outcome the company and/or our boss is trying to achieve,
✔ And where we fit toward achieving that outcome.

## KNOW YOUR CONTRIBUTION

Our work may be meaningful to us and to the community, and we may know our expectations, but we may still be stressed because we don't know if our contribution is appreciated. **What specific skills** do we bring to the table? **What knowledge, experience, or ability** do we bring that is necessary to the success of the endeavor? **What value** do we add to our company or team? These skills are not just task skills but social skills as well. For example:

✔ Do we sense when someone is not being understood, and can we rephrase the person's thoughts so that others will understand?
✔ Perhaps we take complex ideas and simplify them so everyone can grasp the concept.
✔ Perhaps we know how to inject a sense of humor when things are becoming too tense.

I have watched hundreds of people burn out because they did not believe their contribution was acknowledged as valuable not only by their boss, but by co-workers as well. Unfortunately, praise is hard to come by. So, in considering your own contribution to your work, do you know that you are a valuable member of your team? Do you know that you bring skills and abilities that

are needed in your job right now? Think about the work you perform and the interpersonal skills you bring to your job and acknowledge your contribution. I know it would be a lot more helpful if your boss or co-workers would show appreciation without asking for it; however, sometimes that is just not going to happen. In that case, it's important to at least make sure you know you are making a valuable contribution.

## KNOW HOW TO DO YOUR JOB

Another major reason we get stressed at work is because we don't know *how* to do our job or a particular portion of it. You may be very clear about *what* you are supposed to do, just not clear *how* to do it. This, of course, is not just true in your work and career, it is true in your personal life as well. When I am asked to coach someone at the management level, I have rarely found that people don't know *what* they should be doing. It almost always has to do with *how* they do it. When we don't know *how* to accomplish something, it can have an enormously debilitating effect on our self-esteem and our ability to perform.

If you are struggling with your perception that you are not as competent as you would like to be, it helps to take an inventory of your skills. Being bone honest and realistic, ask yourself, "Where am I now and where do I need to be?" Where is the gap? For example, you may not be skilled in the area of information system technology. What will it take, then, to accomplish the needed skills for you to be competitive? In order to feel more competent you can access other more expert resources to help you.

Maybe you are thinking about a different career. What will it take for you to move into that career? Whether you want to improve your competencies within your own job or start a new career what do you need to do?

✔ Take specific classes to maintain competency, or learn new competencies.
✔ Set a goal for yourself so that you will always be in a state of continuous learning.
✔ Read literature.
✔ Read books and magazines in the areas in which you are interested.
✔ Ask questions of those who know.
✔ Find the names of people who are the experts in their field and take them to coffee, breakfast or lunch and ask questions.

Once you have identified the areas that you need to know more about, you can take control and manage your own learning.

## KNOW AND EVALUATE COSTS AND REWARDS OF JOB

Your job may pay you a lot of money, you may know what and how to do it, but is the stress you experience worth it? Do the rewards you receive outweigh the aggravation and lack of fun you experience? It is helpful to make a list of the pros and cons of your present job. What are the rewards versus the costs in mental and physical wear and tear?

I recently visited with a young woman, just 24 years old, who was beset with major physical problems. Through testing, it was discovered that she was under extreme stress at work. She tried to focus on the specific source of her stress and narrowed it down to one co-worker! She loves her job and does not want to quit or move to another department, but she is literally killing herself physically, emotionally and spiritually because of the impact of one co-worker!

For those of us who find ourselves under similar stress, it helps to step back and evaluate the situation. Is the pain short-lived? Does the present job fulfill a short-term personal or professional goal? The point is, do we know and have we clarified, why we are enduring the pain of that present job? Is the reward we will attain really worth the stress?

I've also learned that sometimes a job that creates stress can in itself be addictive. Some people enjoy the adrenaline rush of a lot to do—deadlines, frenzied activity and co-workers who make them angry so they can complain bitterly. Is this stress-related "high" worth it in the long run? Here is one way to find out:

✔ Make a list of present costs and rewards of your job and evaluate them.

✔ Fill out a two-column worksheet defining:

| Costs of present job | Rewards I have received or will receive from present job. |
| --- | --- |
| | |

The reason for this exercise is to be clear in your own mind that it is **YOUR** choice to stay in the job for the reasons you have listed. You can take control of your situation by taking yourself out of the victim role and placing yourself in a proactive role. You may decide that your job isn't that bad, or that the benefits may not be what you want now, but will provide you with necessary skills and benefits for the future. Part of what helps us manage the stress in our lives is knowing that we are in control. I pull my own strings. I can manage myself.

## UPDATE YOUR RESUME

Another way to manage stress is to manage your career options. Part of the reason we experience stress in our professions is because we struggle with believing our career options are limited. Sometimes it is helpful to ask what else you could do if you didn't do what you're presently doing? When we take stock of our skills, experiences and abilities, it's amazing how it opens up other possibilities that we hadn't thought of.

Writing or updating our resume is not only important for possible job opportunities, it also gives us an opportunity to evaluate what we know, our skills and experience. It is a wonderful way to assess how competent we really are. Many people tell me that keeping their resume updated is very comforting and affirming to their self-esteem.

In preparing to write a resume, it is helpful to state the **summary** of your skills and experience at the top. In one or two sentences what do you bring to an organization?

The next section should **list your skills.** What do you bring to an organization that they want? These skills can be listed in bullet form with a very brief description.

Next **list your experience.** This section can be organized according to jobs held, companies for which you have worked, or it can be a descriptive listing of your areas of experience. In thinking about your experiences, it is always important to remember what your have learned.

Sit down with a paper and pencil. Divide the paper into three columns. At the top of the first column write "experiences," above the second column write "skills learned," and for the third column write "meaningfulness." It's helpful to go over all of your

life's experiences from the time you had your first job and the activities you participated in school. In the "experiences" column list all of the tasks you did. Under the second column, or "skills learned," note what those tasks taught you. In the last column, list the ways those skills and experiences were meaningful to you.

For example, as a mother if you stayed home for a period of time to care for small children, what skills are transferable to the workplace? Caring for the children, cleaning, washing, cooking and managing the household taught you how to juggle several tasks at once and accomplish them all with relative ease. You also learned how to have patience.

If in your lifetime you worked part-time as a laborer, you probably learned what it takes to build a product, the need for exact specifications, and the need for communication between all aspects of the organization to ensure that all necessary resources were available to complete the product.

Next comes **education**. If appropriate include **other activities, associations, etc.**

Most people try to keep their resume to two pages. It is important to always think in terms of what we bring to the company, not what the company brings to us. Most recruiters want to know how we can contribute to the job, not what we want to get out of it.

## FINDING THE RIGHT JOB

Many of us have fantasized in our minds about some kind of work that would fulfill a dream. What would be the attributes of this dream job? Make a list of the necessary ingredients such as: varied hours, travel, no contact with customers, contact with customers, working alone, working in teams, adventure, stability, selling a specific product, working with special groups, children, or the elderly. Once you have listed these attributes, you can get a list of all of the job titles from the library reference desk and look for those that appeal to you and/or satisfies your list of important attributes.

When you have a pretty good idea of what you want, a job title that looks appealing, and what your skills and experiences are, find people with those jobs and make an appointment to talk about how they got there. Find out how they accomplished their goal. Find out what education or training they required and use the information to help determine what steps you will have to take to reach your goals. Once you have outlined the required steps, you can develop a plan that will help you get the job of your dreams.

## NETWORKING

It has been said that there is nothing more stressful than looking for a new job. And these days many of us seem to be looking for new jobs continually. Networking means building a web of professional connections with people in various positions and fields who can potentially be resources for us. It includes building a resource base of people to connect with when we need a reference or assistance in finding a new job. Whenever you meet someone interesting, ask for his or her card. The old adage, "It's not what you know, but who you know," is still very true. A recommendation from a specific person who has met us or knows us can be an important entree to a new job.

## PHYSICAL STRETCH BREAKS

No matter what you do physically on your job, you certainly carry the stress of it in your body. Holding that stress in your muscles can be a sure recipe for muscle spasm or strains. Depending upon the degree of stress you may be experiencing it helps to take physical stretch breaks often to help physically

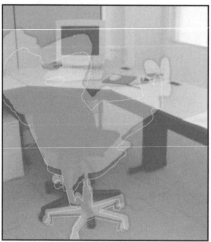

release the stress. We've all heard how important exercising is, but we don't hear how important it is to stretch. Even if your job keeps you physically active and you believe you don't need to stretch, you are mistaken. Even though there are muscles that get used all the time, it's still very important to stretch all of our muscles. Physical therapists encourage us to stretch our muscles at least once a day—more often if we have been in one position for a long period of time. Stretching also helps us relax.

If you work for hours at a time in front of your computer, it's important to take eye breaks every few hours. To avoid eye strain, headaches and other vision problems take an eye break for a few minutes. Relax and focus on far-off objects. Closing your eyes and rolling them around in their sockets also helps.

There are many exercises and activities that help relieve the pressure of repetitive movement and the strain of being in one position for long periods of time. For more information about helpful exercises for work, contact your Human Resource Department.

## REMEMBER, IT'S JUST A JOB!

Our job is not us, it's what we do. If we think we are having a bad day and are becoming more and more stressed, we need to take some advice from the comedian, C. W. Metcalf:

*Walk to the door of your office, cubicle or workstation
and announce that your job, desk or telephone
is having a bad day.*

*Walk away from it until it has a chance to calm down.
Then go back and start again.*

If we treat our job or work as something we do that is separate from who we are, we can take crisis and apparent calamity in stride. Remember, we are in control of our mind and feelings. Our jobs do not control us.

## USE YOUR SENSE OF HUMOR

Have you ever been around someone who is depressed or negative? Not something we look forward to, is it? Ever been around someone who has a wonderful sense of humor or who is light-

•••••••••••••••••••••••••••••••••••••

hearted? What a wonderful way to relieve the stress we're feeling which, in turn, helps us to be more productive.

I have often wished I were funny. I'm not. But I can sure see things that will make me smile or laugh and I can be lighthearted in my approach to work. I can always find something to laugh about in myself. (Seeing myself in the mirror first thing in the morning is pretty hilarious!) It's really all in the perspective. Not only does humor and lightheartedness make the workplace and work more endurable, it really helps us to be more productive.

I have been fortunate to meet many managers, supervisors and employees who have shared the ways they were able to create a more enjoyable workplace.

## ASSIGN A DIRECTOR OF MIRTH

Put someone in charge of mirth or humor every month and give her or him an assignment to come up with things that are funny, humorous, or fun.

## PHYSICAL ENVIRONMENT

Making our work area pleasant for us is very important. Since we are at work so much of the time, it helps to put our personality into our space—our favorite pictures on the wall, inspirational poems, plants, flowers, cartoons and, if possible, music. Sometimes, it is also necessary to change your work area around. Think of this space as your home away from home. What can you do to make your surroundings more enjoyable?

Your car is another important space. Is your car *driver friendly?* Do you have the right tapes or CD's? Do you have writing materials so when you think of things you can jot them down? Is your car fun to drive?

It may not seem important, but the physical spaces we're in do a lot toward helping us relieve some of our tension and stress.

# Having Fun While We Work

- Make a conscious effort to lighten up.

- Plan to have fun things to do during the day.

- Plant post it notes around your office with fun sayings on them.

- Sing songs together.

- Have stuffed toys that people can carry around with them.

- Make joy lists.

- Have Koosh basketball games or Nerfball table tennis tournaments.

- Have a comic break—bring in videos of comedy situations.

- Put up funny art from time to time.

- Have internal silly contests.

- Give out silly awards—best hair, best pair of socks.

- Have large pieces of paper on doors of offices for people to draw pictures and leave notes or cartoons.

- Have costume days when it's not Halloween—perhaps to commemorate other holidays (e.g., dressing in a heart costume on Valentine's Day, an Easter Bunny on Easter).

- Have dress up and dress down days.

- Have contests for the best cartoon or joke.

- Have fun First Aid Kits.

- Give everyone on your team a special title.

# Find Light-Hearted Ways to Say Things

■ Find fun ways of communicating with your co-workers and boss.

■ Write memos in the form of movie reviews.

■ Use different colors to get people's attention.

■ Deliver tedious information with an accent.

■ Develop a different persona to deliver news—Sherlock Holmes, Dick Tracy, Roseanne, Captain Kirk, or Doctor Spock from the Starship Enterprise.

# Making Meetings Fun

■ Create a whine down period, or a whine and cheese event, to allow co-workers to vent frustrations of the day— approximately 5 to 10 minutes is enough. Use a clock.

■ Bring food.

■ Have on-going games with prizes.

■ Wear different colored hats depending upon the thinking requirements of the various meetings: e.g., blue for creative brainstorming, green for problem solving, yellow for information sharing or red for crisis decision time.

# Show Appreciation to Co-Workers

■ Give fun rewards for helping each other with projects.

■ Make signs that say, "Thank You."

■ Give humorous gifts.

- Recognize co-workers with "queen or king for a day." Roll out a special carpet, bring coffee, wait on that person.

- Develop a wall of fame.

- Give personalized T-shirts or hats.

- Use "uh-oh" awards when people make mistakes, have a best "uh-oh" award for the quarter.

## GIVE YOURSELF SCHMOOZE BREAKS

The *Harvard Business Review*, (1976, June/July issue,) defined *schmoozing* as taking a little informal, mini-break. The word comes from Yiddish and is used to describe chit-chat or "chewing the fat." It may be the meet-and-greet session before an event or a dinner. It is usually informal but involves information gathering/ sharing and gossip and can be a means of networking. It is meant to be relaxing, a kind of break in the intensity of work.

When we have been working intensely at a task for a period of time, a trigger goes off inside that says, "It's time for a little break." Usually it is impossible to take a formal break; but we might go to the bathroom or get a drink of water, and on our way chit-chat with others. This little break allows our brain a chance to reorganize itself and to come back to the task with renewed vigor and concentration.

## TAKE MINI-VACATIONS

It is also important to take mini-vacations. Think of something every day that you can look forward to with pleasure. It never needs to be much or take a great deal of time. Maybe it's a walk or workout, a special program on television, an opportunity to read your favorite book, a special lunch or dinner or just sitting quietly enjoying the sunset. Make a special time every day that is your mini-vacation.

Take yourself to lunch, the museum, an art gallery or the park. Pretend you are a tourist once a week and take yourself out to see the sights. Whatever you do, inject an element of fun and adventure. Consider it your little vacation for the day.

**References:**
Many of the previous ideas come from *301 Ways to Have Fun at Work* by Dave Hemsath and Leslie Yerkes.

Covey, Stephen R. *Principled Centered Leadership.*

Covey, Stephen R. *7 Habits of Highly Effective People.*

Nelson, Bob. *1001 Ways to Reward Employees.*

Davidson, Stephanie Goddard. *101 Ways to Have a Great Day at Work.*

Mauer, Rick. *Feedback Toolkit.* The author gives a very good model to use in giving feedback.

Booher, Dianna. *Get a Life Without Sacrificing Your Career.*

# TENDING THE SOUL
## The Ultimate Source of Wholeness

*The soul is made of love and must ever strive to return to love.*
*Therefore, it can never find rest nor happiness in other things.*
*It must lose itself in love.*
*By its very nature it must seek God, who is love.*
Mechthild of Magdeburg

*At the center of our being is a point of nothingness*
*which is untouched by sin and by illusion, a point of*
*pure truth, a point or spark which belongs entirely to God,*
*which is never at our disposal, from which God*
*disposes of our lives, which is inaccessible to the fantasies*
*of our own mind or the brutalities of our own will.*
Thomas Merton

This book is about how to manage stress and burnout and find wholeness and balance in our lives. You may wonder what talking about the soul has to do with managing stress and burnout. Actually, a lot! When I refer to the soul, I do not mean a religious interpretation of a doctrine or belief. I'm referring to that indefinable place within that provides us the inner resources to go on.

Recently, I had a very intense conversation with a dear friend diagnosed with a rare lung cancer. I asked him how he was able to survive the intensive chemotherapy, its devastating side effects plus all of the continuing and ongoing demands of life. He said that he had a deep sense of optimism and hope, and an element of adventure and curiosity about this new, and maybe final, chapter of his life. His comments struck me because there are many times when I have no idea what will happen to me. However, there is this uncanny resource within me that I sense is assuring and reassuring me that all will be well. Although I am not coping with a terminal disease, I, too, have experienced a sense of curiosity wondering how it will all turn out. In my darkest hours when I feel enormously afraid, there still is that deep sense of hope or knowledge that I will get through it. As Thomas Merton says in the above quote, "there is a point of nothingness within that no one can touch."

One way to access that powerful inner resource is through daily quiet times.

## QUIET TIME

Personal power and control come from learning how to experience calm in our deepest self by spending time every day being quiet. I am firmly convinced that the greatest power we have at our disposal is not found outside of ourselves, but within. And the only way to access that power is to go inside. A quiet time means that we are alone in a quiet place with no distractions with one purpose—to connect with our inner resources, our inner self.

Start by sitting in a chair or on a bed, someplace comfortable with your back well supported. Close your eyes and take very deep breaths. (If it is impossible for you to be someplace quiet, you can use headphones with meditative music or nature sounds to help shut out distractions. You can also buy very inexpensive ear plugs from the grocery store.)

Sometimes it is helpful to focus on a certain word to increase concentration. Or, if you are troubled and anxious and need a way to focus, there are effective ways to breathe and use words to help bring peacefulness to your spirit. For example, say:

*"I breathe in peace, breathe out anger."*
*"I breathe in joy, breathe out sadness."*
*"I breathe in love, breathe out hatred."*
*"I breathe in hope, breathe out fear."*

Whatever is frightening you, stressing you, or seems negative, breathe it out and breathe in the energy that will renew your spirit. You can also use a word like "peace" or a personal affirmation like "I am loveable" to center yourself. You might find it helpful to slowly repeat a phrase like "calm down," "let go," or "I am safe" over and over. During your quiet time find a statement that is especially comforting to you.

I can't stress how important it is to set aside some quiet time every day. It's the daily ritual that makes a difference. Start with ten minutes a day. This does not mean to imply that the entire ten minutes will be productive. Most of us have times when we fidget, daydream, drift, or feel bored. During my own quiet time I sometimes think to myself, "how stupid" or "who am I kidding?" If this happens to you, don't give up! Something that helps me stay on track is to keep a piece of paper handy so I can write down any thoughts that interrupt me. Then I can put aside those thoughts knowing I can come back to them later.

If you practice your Quiet Time every day, one day you will have a split second or a brief moment when SOMETHING HAPPENS! That something is the connection to your deepest core—it is an awareness, a knowing, without knowing why you know. It is a kind of awakening whereby you know that you GOT IT! At that moment you will feel a profound sense of quiet and peace. That moment will also start an addictive process for you whereby you will not be satisfied until you can duplicate the experience again and again.

If you go on day after day and nothing happens, just keep trying. If you find yourself getting anxious, you are defeating the purpose. Remember to keep your back straight and if you start to doze, sit away from the back of the chair or the bed. The idea is to be comfortable, but not so comfortable that it induces sleep. And if you fall asleep, it doesn't help to beat yourself up. You're just relaxed and that's okay. If you find yourself getting frustrated and anxious, it doesn't help to concentrate or focus on the frustration. Just breathe deeply for ten minutes and leave it at that. Whatever you do, don't stop the practice. Remember, practice makes perfect.

### Quiet Time Break

Very often during the day we need a break from the chaos to calm ourselves down. During these times, meditation tapes may be useful, a short walk may help, sitting alone for awhile and not talking will also help. We may want to read some poetry, some favorite verses, or listen to quiet music. It matters not, as long as we have some time quietly alone.

### Communion with God, Higher Power, Divine

There are many ways to pray to God. (For ease of writing, I will refer to whatever our/your notion is of a Supreme Being as God.) Intercessory prayer is praying for others. Prayer of repentance is asking for forgiveness for something for which we are sorry. Prayer for guidance and direction is asking for help in specific problems we are facing. Contemplative prayer is being in communion with God.

For some of us, finding the source of serenity and calm and release from stress comes from being in communion with God, or quietly sitting in that inner place where God is. Communing with God also occurs while walking, working or being engaged in any activity in life. It's being aware of God's presence always within.

## MAKE YOUR OWN INTERNAL SANCTUARY

In order for us to find it easier to be quiet and go inward, it helps to develop our own internal sanctuary. We can make this place really special by closing our eyes and visualizing the perfect "Quiet Place" for us. Imagine how large it is. What kind of paint or wallpaper does it have? What pictures are on the wall? What kind of table and chairs are in it? Where is the most comfortable place to sit? Do we have all of our very special "stuff" close by? What candles are burning? Maybe our special sanctuary is a place

 by the ocean, or a place in the mountains or any other place that brings us peace and calm. My special place is on the Oregon Coast. Whenever I have my quiet time, I often go to that wonderful place and sit quietly in there to help me gain my composure and control.

## PERSONAL SYMBOLS

When we are under great stress, seeing a visual reminder of a time, place or special memory, will often have the effect of actually being in that peaceful and happy moment and can be very comforting. It helps to go back over our lives and try to remember the times when we were the most happy, satisfied, clear about who we were, content and peaceful. Maybe it was when we were on a special vacation with our family, a friend, or even alone. Maybe it was a time when we were a volunteer and contributed something that we knew made a real difference. What was that time or event that was so meaningful to us? Bring it to our memory and try to remember what it was about that time that brought us so much joy. What was the difference for us? Why were we different then? What was the magical combination that made that special time so meaningful? A wonderful example of this concept is expressed in W. P. Kinsella's *Shoeless Joe*:

*"What is this magic you keep talking about? It's the place and the time. The right place and right time. A time when all the cosmic tumblers have clicked into place and the universe opens up for a few seconds, or hours, and shows you what is possible. And then you not only see, but hear, and smell, and taste, and touch whatever is closest to your heart's desire. Your secret dreams that grow over the years like apple seeds sown in your belly, grow up through you in leafy wonder and finally sprout through your skin, gentle and soft and wondrous, and they breathe and have a life of their own."*

•••••••••••••••••••••••••••••••••••••••••

Naming all of our "tumblers" helps us to realize that those resources are there for us now. Although at the time that moment of joy may have seemed like an "accident," it doesn't mean that it cannot be duplicated through remembering.

After we have spent some time thinking about those special times and events in our lives, we can make a symbol or use something that will visibly remind us of that special time. It may be a photograph, picture or painting of that special vacation, or time alone in the mountains or at the beach. It may be poem, a saying, a momento, a crystal, a necklace, a belt buckle, whatever it might be, have it visible so that it will always remind you of that special time or special memory.

In the midst of a hectic day when I am suddenly feeling all of the stress symptoms, it helps to have some type of visual symbol as a reminder of those times when I really felt connected, whole and serene. Sometimes it's a special picture, thinking of my family or friends, or my new granddaughter.

## SURRENDERING/LETTING GO

*God grant me the serenity to accept the things I cannot change,*
*The courage to change the things I can,*
*And the wisdom to know the difference.*
Serenity Prayer by Reinhold Niebuhr

Once again, the meaning of the Serenity Prayer is powerful. It is powerful to me because I find when I'm the most stressed it's because I want to control not only my own little world, but also *the* world. If only I were president! I could certainly influence things differently! I cannot change those things or people in my surroundings. The only *person* I can control is myself and the only *things* I can control are those things which are directly caused by me.

Being able to surrender sounds good, but what does it mean and how does one do it? And how does it relate to my soul? Surrendering control is the ability to stop taking responsibility and accountability for how every outcome is received. It is knowing that when I do the right thing, live from my values of what is right and wrong, the outcome will generally take care of itself. Of course, it is very important that we are clear on where our responsibility begins and ends, what we truly have control of and what we do not.

I try to do all the things I have shared with you in this book. I take care of myself physically, manage my emotions, tend to my spirit needs, keep challenging my mind, nurture my relationships and find a great deal of meaning in my work. In spite of that, there are times when I have been in the bottom of the barrel of near hopelessness. When I have my quiet time every day and remember that I am guided by a Divine Source and that if I let go of my control and follow God's guidance, all will be well. I also am reminded that when I'm paying attention to how great spiritual teachers and leaders lived and loved, I will have a better chance to find peace if I practice the same.

## LIVING A LOVING LIFE

Regardless of what all of the religions espouse, I have found that the real relief from stress comes when I am loving and kind to others. For many, this kind of commitment is too demanding and shows weakness. However, the most personally powerful people I know are incredibly kind and loving to everyone! What does it mean to live a "loving" life?

Since very few of us are like a Mother Theresa, Gandhi, or Saint Frances of Assisi, what does living a loving life mean? Jesus talked about how we should behave to one another that is pretty radical. He was fairly odd and revolutionary in his teaching of how God expects us to behave to others. Religious leaders, through the trickery of teaching about doctrine or interpretations of what Jesus and other spiritual teachers have said, have skirted around the real truth.

Some of the things that pertain to how we are to live with each other are:

- We are to live meek and humbly—not ego centered.
- We are to be peacemakers.
- We are to do good deeds.
- We are not to judge others.
- We are not to be sexually promiscuous.
- We are not to get even with those who hurt or harm us.
- We are to love our enemies and those who are very unlike us.
- We are not to show off and brag about our good deeds—again not being ego-centered.
- We are to commune with God.

## BEING MEEK AND HUMBLE

The connotation of being meek and humble is one that conjures up wimpiness. Anyone who is meek is a person with no spine who lets people walk all over them. These are people we do not want to align ourselves with because they annoy us. We want to be with people who are powerful, have money, status and influence. But what does meek and humble really mean? It means that we get our ego out of the way. Most of the trouble we find ourselves in—financial difficulties, relationship problems, problems at work, when we have lied, or any other problem—is directly related to protecting our ego. When we worry about our looks, about what others think, whether we make an impression – all of those nonproductive attitudes and behaviors are directly traced to wanting to enhance our own ego. Great spiritual teachers tell us that the way to find peace and joy is to let go of our ego.

What do you need to do in your life to live more simply and humbly? The more you seek for material wealth the more stressful you become with worries. Letting go of ego also helps you to let go of trying to prove yourself sexually, financially, physically and intellectually.

## PEACEMAKING

Another requisite for happiness is being a peacemaker. This means always finding ways to resolve conflict, not make it. How can you be a part of making peace within your family, your community, at work, in the country and in the world? This does not mean that you must tolerate evil. It means that you look for ways to bring about resolution to differences instead of allowing disharmony to exist. To find ways to resolve conflict, review the material in Chapter 5.

## DOING GOOD DEEDS

Spiritual teachers tell us how important it is to do good deeds for others. It is not enough to talk about them; what is important is that we do them. What do you do to give to others? Many of us give to be seen and recognized rather than for the pure joy of giving. We may give out of "have to" rather than "want to." Deep down we all know what doing good means. What does doing good mean for you?

## NOT JUDGING OTHERS

Have you ever tried to go for two hours and not judge anyone? Of all the things that we are told to do, this seems to be the most impossible and one that seems so illogical. If we didn't judge, there would be no law, there would be no evaluation of what others do in terms of what is right or wrong by legal and moral standards. So what does "not judging" mean? Our fragile egos must have constant care and feeding, therefore, they stack themselves up against what other people do. Our egos feel better when they can compare and compete with others on the basis that others are worse and we are better. We are told that we will be much happier, have a lot less stress when we stop competing and comparing ourselves to others.

## NOT BEING SEXUALLY PROMISCUOUS

Not only does sexual promiscuity outside of a meaningful relationship lead to a greater possibility of venereal disease, the sexual act is highly intimate and personal; and taking one's clothes off can leave one very vulnerable. All of us know, in our souls, where the line is in being promiscuous. Pay attention to your inner voice and live the way that is right for you.

## NOT GETTING EVEN

One of the hardest things to do when someone has hurt us deeply, is to not think of a way to get even. There is a fine line between exacting consequences and getting even. Not getting even means letting go of the anger and rage you feel over the injustices done to you. There are times when consequences must be expected, but after the consequences, then what? Let go of the negative energy that might be consuming you by writing down all of your hateful thoughts. Keep writing the hate and rage out on paper until you finally feel some relief. Review the section of how to write things down in Chapter 5.

## LOVING OUR ENEMIES

Great spiritual leaders set the challenge before us to love others. I find that the challenge to love our enemies is the most difficult challenge facing any of us today. It's easy to show love to people we already like. We are asked to show love to people we don't like. We are asked to make loving the cornerstone of our lives and essence. Why? Because loving makes us feel better—

not only physically, but emotionally and spiritually. Loving is like putting a soothing ointment on a raw sore. It is like being curled up safe and warm when everything outside is scary and cold. Love is healing. It is the only thing that is totally healing inside and out.

That challenge is pretty tough to do. How do you love someone who is doing evil deeds? How do you love someone who is full of hatred? Spiritual teachers tell us that anyone can love someone who is handsome or nice, pretty, or gentle. How can we love people who are not pretty, who are unpleasant, who are cruel? It is certainly not easy. For most of us, it's impossible! But think of it this way. What happens when you hate someone? What does it do to you to hate? Remember the discussion of how fear and anger can destroy our immune system? Hatred consumes us like a poison and destroys us. And the only real antidote to hatred is loving.

## Not Bragging About Ourselves

I have never heard or read of great spiritual teachers and leaders bragging about themselves. While it is important to care for ourselves and develop strong positive self-esteem, there is a big difference between that and arrogance. When someone brags about him- or herself, what is the first thought that occurs to us? Generally, we are aware that the person is very insecure. If we have a need to brag, we need to ask ourselves what of our five needs: self-esteem, security, competency, trust and love, is missing? Because if we are bragging, there is a good probability that one of our five needs is not being fulfilled and we are seeking recognition and fulfillment. Review Chapter 6 on how the needs of the spirit can be met in order to reduce stress.

## Reflection as the Tool to Provide Insight and Discernment

In order for us to grow and understand the needs of our spirit, we must be able to reflect. Wisdom and insight come when we spend time reflecting on our inner needs, when we perceive, reflect and judge what is happening in the present moment. It is not only the ability to see, hear and attend to what is happening, but to understand what is going on and why we are being affected by it. By being sensitive and aware of our inner cues, we learn ways to accommodate our spirit needs in healthy and productive ways.

Learn to always ask yourself "why?" "Why am I responding in this way to that person right now?" "Why am I feeling good right now?" "Why did I do or say that?" "What's going on with me right now?" When you begin to ask reflective questions you gather information that gives you insight into what is happening with you at deeper levels. You become much more in tune with your stress triggers and can monitor them more consistently.

## Where To Go From Here

So there you have it! I have tried to give you some ideas about how stress happens, how it leads to burnout and some ways to create wholeness in the seven areas of your life. Obviously, trying to do all of it is overwhelming and would take years of concentrated work. I encourage you to find one or two things to start with. Integrate those changes in your life, first. Then, as you will, add new behaviors to your life. Practice with some of these ideas. I guarantee that you will find yourself more in charge of yourself, more self empowered with a new sense of joy and wholeness!

I remind you that managing stress is never a "done deal." It is every day living and reminding yourself of some of the coping methods you would like to try. No doubt you will start something and then lose interest and forget about it until you get stressed and sick and then remember some of the things that were talked about. Don't give up. Don't beat yourself up. This is a journey and it takes a lot of practice.

Please keep in touch with me by email: dkercher@aol.com. Tell me some of the things that were particularly helpful to you. Let me know what you would like me to add to the next edition and I will make the additions and give you credit. We will make this a nation-wide project with all of us working together to help each other manage stress and burnout while we're "Juggling as Fast as We Can!"

**References:** Williamson, Marianne. *A Return to Love.* A very insightful book on the power of love and loving.

Capra, Fritjof. *The Web of Life.* A discussion of how all of life is interconnected.

Armstrong, Karen. *A History of God.* An excellent book about how the three traditions—Christianity, Judaism and Islam—came from the same roots.

Hanh, Thich Nhat. *Peace is Every Step.* Hanh is a Buddhist monk with wonderful suggestions on how to live and be in the present.

Muller, Wayne. *Sabbath.* This is a wonderful book on the importance of taking time to be quiet, to stop work activity and find ways to rest and relax.

Kidd, Sue Monk. *When the Heart Waits.* Another wonderful book on the importance of listening to your inner voice.

Easwaran, Eknath. *On Meditation.* Very helpful book on learning how to meditate and get quiet.

Other books that have been incredibly helpful to me are books written by Father Thomas Keating and Father Thomas Merton. They particularly focus on centering and contemplative prayer. I have found their works to be very comforting.

*I claim to be an average man of less than average ability. I have not the shadow of a doubt that any man or woman can achieve what I have, if he or she would make the same effort and cultivate the same hope and faith.*

Mahatma Gandhi

*...If we are to leave a peaceful and healthy earth for our children, it will be the ordinary man and woman who do it; not by becoming extraordinary, but by discovering that our greatest strength lies not in how much we differ from each other but in how much—how very much—we are the same.*

Eknath Easwaran

### People Who Have Active Mastery Over Their Lives
### from Deepak Chopra

People who have mastery over their lives:

- Know how to deal with toxins in their lives
  (physical, emotional, spiritual).

- Shed, at the deepest level, the need to gain approval
  and to control.

- Use mirror of relationships for their own growth and
  evolution.

- Experience themselves through the core of their own
  being.

- Are in touch with their physical bodies.

- Are grounded in the present.

- Have relinquished need to judge others.

- Replace fear-based behavior with love-based behavior.

- See the whole universe as a projection of themselves

WE ARE what we eat, how we behave, and how we think.